D0201176

TRIUMPH AND TERROR

Otfinoski, Steven.
Triumph and terror : the
French Revolution /
c1993.
33305004332809
CA   10/20/95

TRIUMPH AND TERROR

The French Revolution

STEVEN OTFINOSKI

Facts On File

SANTA CLARA COUNTY LIBRARY

3 3305 00433 2809

Triumph and Terror: The French Revolution

Copyright © 1993 by Steven Otfinoski

All rights reserved. No part of this book may be reproduced or utilized in any form or by any means, electronic or mechanical, including photocopying, recording, or by any information storage or retrieval systems, without permission in writing from the publisher. For information contact:

Facts On File, Inc.
460 Park Avenue South
New York NY 10016
USA

Library of Congress Cataloging-in-Publication Data

Otfinoski, Steven.
    Triumph and terror : the French Revolution / Steven Otfinoski.
      p. cm.   — (World history library)
    Includes bibliographical references and index.
    Summary: Discusses the causes, events, and aftermath of the
revolution that began in 1789 with the overthrow of the monarchy and
ended ten years later with the rise of the Napoleonic dictatorship.
    ISBN 0-8160-2762-5
    1. France—History—Revolution, 1789–1799—Juvenile literature.
[1. France—History—Revolution, 1789–1799.] I. Title.
II. Series.
DC148.088   1993
944.04—dc20   92-37131

A British CIP catalogue record for this book is available from the British Library.

Facts On File books are available at special discounts when purchased in bulk quantities for businesses, associations, institutions or sales promotions. Please contact our Special Sales Department in New York at 212/683-2244 (dial 800/322- 8755 except in NY).

Series design by Donna Sinisgalli
Cover design by Amy Gonzalez
Composition by Facts On File/Robert Yaffe
Manufactured by the Maple-Vail Book Manufacturing Group
Printed in the United States of America

10 9 8 7 6 5 4 3 2 1

This book is printed on acid-free paper.

CONTENTS

INTRODUCTION

Revolution. The very word conjures up peasants storming the palace gates, kings fleeing for their lives, a corrupt system of government crumbling and a new and just order taking its place. Webster defines revolution as "a complete and forcible overthrow of an established government or political system."

Few revolutions in modern times have fulfilled that definition better than the one that began in France in 1789. The American Revolution that took place a few years earlier established a new nation; the French Revolution established a new order for an old world—Europe. Its repercussions were felt on that continent for well over a century.

The French Revolution, like other great events of history, is misunderstood by many people today. They remember it only for the storming of the Bastille and the bloody Reign of Terror. But between these two momentous events many things happened that changed our understanding of just what a revolution is.

Revolutions, we are told, are supposed to be swift and decisive. But the French Revolution lasted from six to ten years, depending on which historian you read. Within that span there were periods of turmoil, civil insurrection, war, anarchy, order and relative peace. Numerous charismatic leaders, several legislative bodies and a succession of constitutions came and went during these years. There were actually several revolutions—not one—and each was more radical and violent than the one preceding it.

Revolutions are supposed to herald the triumph of the poor and underprivileged over the rich and powerful. In truth, the events that led to the French Revolution were set in motion by dissatisfied members of the aristocracy and then taken over by the middle class. Only later did the poor seize power. Although the masses emerged as a powerful force in the Revolution, they were almost always under the control of intellectuals, lawyers and journalists.

Revolutions are supposed to create a new social order based on equality, brotherhood and harmony. The French Revolution, for all its sound and fury, established no utopia on earth. When the Revolution ended, power largely lay in the hands of the people who had been consolidating it before the old regime collapsed—primarily the merchants, generals and bureaucrats of France.

What kind of a revolution was this then? Despite the inconsistencies just noted, it was one that greatly changed the "natural order" of Europe. The French Revolution was not just a revolt against the regime of the Bourbon kings—it embodied an entire new way of viewing the world and human society. Although the Revolution failed to live up to its own rallying cry of "liberty, equality and fraternity," it spread these ideals far and wide. They have made our world what it is today.

EVE OF
DESTRUCTION

"L'Etat c'est moi." (I am the state.)
–Louis XIV

It all began with money. The king needed it, the nobles and the middle class didn't want to give it to him, and the poor didn't have it to give.

Louis XVI, the king of France, felt he had every right to tax whomever he pleased. After all, his family, the Bourbons, had ruled France by "the divine right of God" for 200 years. The royal dynasty had reached the peak of its power during the long reign of Louis XIV, "the Sun King," from 1643 to 1715. Louis had masterfully dealt with the age-old threat of his ambitious nobles by creating a fairy-tale palace at Versailles, just outside Paris, the capital. There lords and their ladies came from their ancestral estates, to live as impotent courtiers under the king's watchful eye.

Louis XIV may have been the master of France, but he was also the overseer of its financial ruin. With affairs secure at home, Louis waged a series of disastrous wars with his neighbors for power and territory. His great-grandson, Louis XV, who ascended the throne in 1715, spent

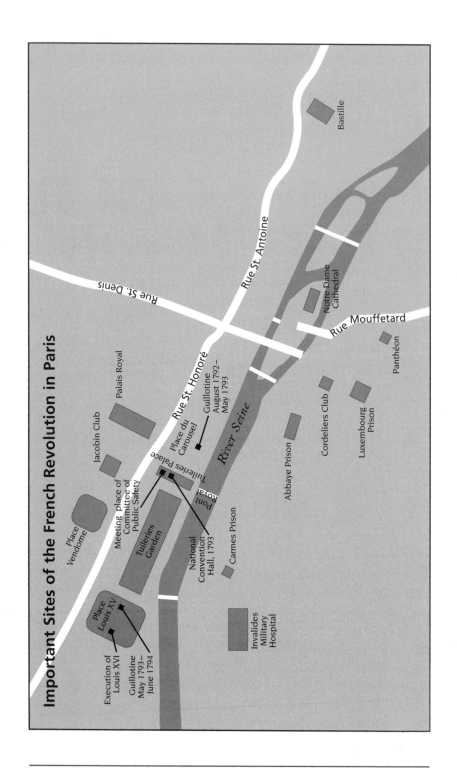

Important Sites of the French Revolution in Paris

Place Vendôme
Jacobin Club
Palais Royal
Meeting place of Committee of Public Safety
Tuileries Garden
Tuileries Palace
Place du Carousel
Rue St. Honoré
Guillotine August 1792– May 1793
River Seine
Pont Royal
National Convention Hall, 1793
Carmes Prison
Place Louis XV
Execution of Louis XVI
Guillotine May 1793– June 1794
Invalides Military Hospital
Abbaye Prison
Cordeliers Club
Luxembourg Prison
Panthéon
Rue Mouffetard
Notre Dame Cathedral
Rue St. Antoine
Rue St. Denis
Bastille

money as fast as his predecessor but lacked Louis XIV's gift for state building. Louis XV's profligacy and scandalous personal behavior earned him the loathing of nobles and commoners alike. But Louis cared little for what anyone thought of him. He is best remembered for his brazen declaration, "After me, the deluge!" Even he didn't realize how prophetic those words would be.

In 1774 Louis XVI, Louis XV's grandson, came to power. Unlike his grandfather, he was a man of personal integrity and virtue. Unfortunately, he was also a weak and indecisive ruler. At first, this did not seem a problem. Louis XVI was blessed with a series of gifted and progressive ministers, who saw the country was headed for bankruptcy and tried to do something about it. Robert Turgot and Jacques Necker were two of the most outstanding of Louis's financial managers. They proposed new taxes for the rich nobility and high clergy. But neither of these groups were about to give up their wealth and privileges any more than was the king himself and his extravagant wife, Queen Marie-Antoinette. Despite his promise to support his ministers, Louis abandoned each of them in the face of opposition from the nobles. Meanwhile, the country's debts continued to mount. France's support of America in its revolution against Great Britain was what finally bankrupted the treasury. Ironically, by helping America economically and militarily to win its independence, France moved itself closer to the precipice of its own revolution.

The American Revolution inspired liberal French aristocrats and intellectuals. For the first time they saw that ideals of democracy and justice could work in the real world. Architects of the American republic, such as Thomas Jefferson and Benjamin Franklin, were in turn inspired by such French thinkers as Charles Louis de Montesquieu, Denis Diderot and Voltaire. In their writings, these Frenchmen sharply criticized the old order of kingly power and laid the blueprint for new, more democratic forms of government.

No writer stirred the blood of thinking Frenchmen more than Jean-Jacques Rousseau. While Montesquieu argued for a constitutional monarchy modeled after the English system of government, Rousseau called for more sweeping changes. Rousseau declared that "the general will" of the people should determine who would rule and how. He broke with a thousand years of civilization by celebrating the nobility of more "primitive" societies and the innocence of childhood. "Man is born free, but everywhere he is in chains!" Rousseau boldly proclaimed in his most famous work, *The Social Contract.*

The chains that imprisoned France's growing middle class were largely ones of political restraint. Despite their relative economic wealth, this group had no vote or say in government. For the great masses of peasants, farmers and city workers, however, the chains were far crueler. The peasants were the largest segment of the population, and they lived lives of grinding poverty. What little they earned was greatly diminished by a bewildering array of taxes and church tithes. They even paid a tax for having been born! Peasants lived on small farms rented from an aristocratic landlord. Each year they had to give him ten days of free labor, as well as an annual portion of their crop. Their sons had to serve compulsory terms in the military. Their fields were trampled regularly by wild boars or deer that were under royal protection and could not be killed. And if a peasant was caught killing a game bird to feed his starving family, his punishment was death. It was a brutish way of life that had remained largely unchanged for a thousand years. But the medieval world that had given it birth was coming apart at the seams.

Louis XVI's finance minister, Charles Alexandre de Calonne, had a plan he believed could save the country from bankruptcy. In August 1786 he presented his reform plan to Louis. It called for a general tax on all land to be fairly assessed by assemblies in each province. The delegates of the assemblies would be duly elected by the local land-owners. The king called for the Assembly of Notables—a governing body of the 144 nobles, clerics and government officials—to consider Calonne's proposal. The Assembly had not met since 1626, which shows how often the monarchy consulted with the nobility on matters of importance. Now the Assembly, however, realized how desperate the king was and savored its new power. It flatly rejected the proposed tax.

Once again the king caved in to pressure from the nobility and his own family and dismissed Calonne. Calonne's successor, Archbishop Loménie de Brienne, tried to get through a modified tax plan, but that too was rejected. Thwarted and frustrated, Louis dissolved the Assembly. This led to what has come to be called "The Revolt of the Nobility."

The plight of the Third Estate in pre-Revolutionary France is graphically depicted in this contemporary cartoon. The king, in full regalia, rides a shackled peasant like a beast of burden. Along for the ride are a bishop and a member of Parlement, representing the First and Second estates. (The Bettmann Archive)

In May 1788 the parlement of Paris, the highest court of appeal in the land, denounced the king's despotism in a declaration. This denunciation was a selfish act of the privileged few, cloaked under the guise of defending the "rights" of all the people.

The Marquis de Lafayette, a liberal aristocrat who had fought in the American Revolution, called for the gathering of the Estates-General

JEAN-JACQUES ROUSSEAU (1712-1778)

During the debate over the first French Constitution in August 1789, one deputy of the National Assembly suggested that Rousseau's *Social Contract* be printed at the head of the document. This was hardly a whimsical suggestion. More than any other writer or thinker of the 18th century, Rousseau can claim the title of the Father of the French Revolution.

Rousseau's entire life was a rebellion against "the age of reason" in which he lived. His mother died giving birth to him in Geneva, Switzerland in 1712. At the age of ten, he was abandoned by his father, a watchmaker. As a teenager he took

Rousseau's writings reflect a love of nature and the individual, a celebration of the emotions and a revolt against reason and established authority. He is the spiritual father of both the French Revolution and the Romantic Movement that swept across Europe in the early 19th century. (The New York Public Library Picture Collection)

to consider the issue of taxation. Like the Assembly of Notables, this representative body hadn't been called together for a long time—175 years. Unlike the Assembly, the Estates-General represented not only the nobility—the Second Estate—but the other two classes, or "estates," of French society. These were the First Estate, the Catholic clergy, whose hierarchy enjoyed the same privileges as the nobles, and the Third Estate, which included everyone else. This grab bag of

to the road and tried a number of trades, including servant to a rich family and copier of musical scores. For ten years Rousseau lived with an older wealthy widow. Then he abandoned her and went to Paris.

There he wrote "Discourses on the Sciences and the Arts," an essay that won him a prize and instant fame. In it Rousseau condemned advances in technology and culture, calling them corruptive forces for humankind. In a second essay he depicted the modern political state and its institutions as a prison for the human spirit. To liberate themselves, Rousseau believed people had to reject the modern world and return to their "natural state" by emulating children and more supposedly "primitive" peoples.

Such a philosophy was considered nothing short of treason, and when Rousseau added the Catholic Church to his targets, he was driven into exile. But even in the more liberal climate of England, Rousseau didn't fit in. Like his later disciple Maximilien Robespierre, he imagined conspiracies against him wherever he looked, and his paranoia cost him many friendships. Rousseau returned to Paris with his common-law wife in 1771 and spent his last years in solitary poverty. One of his final works was a draft of a constitution for Poland, requested by a Polish count.

Rousseau's reputation was reborn in the 1780s as a new generation of Frenchmen discovered him. A dozen years after his death, his belief that government should serve "the general will" of the people gave birth to both the best and worst impulses of the French Revolution.

humanity, numbering 25 million[1], ranged from middle-class merchants and lawyers to dirt-poor peasants and laborers. The one thing they shared in common was a complete lack of say in how their country should be run.

1. The first two estates together numbered only 500,000 people. Thus they represented a little less than 2 percent of the population.

But the king was in no mood to have his will subverted. He rejected the idea of calling the Estates-General and ordered the arrest of two ringleaders in the parlement of Paris in May 1788. The nobles responded by agitating the people to riot and protest. The discontented people needed little encouragement.

The results were predictable. The king reluctantly gave in and agreed to summon the Estates-General for the following May. But he put two stipulations on the meeting. First, he insisted the body convene not in Paris, a hotbed of discontent, but at Versailles, where he could remain in firm control of the proceedings and not miss his favorite pastime—hunting. He also agreed, under the urging of the newly recalled Jacques Necker, to double the number of deputies for the Third Estate from the traditional 300 to 600. This would equal the representation of the first two estates combined. Thus, in one cunning stroke Louis and his minister weakened the nobles' power and strengthened the king's influence among the people. They now saw Louis as their champion. In fact, he was using the people for his own ends, just as the nobles had done earlier during their "revolt."

Louis's confidence in the outcome of the Estates-General is reflected in the royal decree issued on August 8, 1788:

> . . . Certain of reaping the fruit of the representatives' enthusiasms and love, His Majesty is already looking forward to calm and peaceful days after the storm, to seeing order restored in all the provinces, to the national debt being consolidated and to France enjoying without disturbance, the power and respect due to its size, population, wealth and the character of its people.

In actuality, the meeting of the Estates-General would not disperse the dark clouds that hung over France. Instead, it would unleash a storm of such fury as the country had not seen since Julius Caesar's invasion of Gaul (the ancient name for France) more than 1,800 years earlier.

CHAPTER 1 NOTES

p. 8   ". . . Certain of reaping the fruit . . ." Richard Cobb and Colin Jones, *Voices of the French Revolution*, p. 26.

SUMMER OF
DISCONTENT

"What is it [the Third Estate] asking for? To become SOMETHING . . . But the Third Estate, it will be said, cannot form the Estates General. All the better! It will compose a National Assembly."
> —Abbé Sieyès in his pamphlet "What Is the Third Estate?" (1789)

While the king saw the meeting of the Estates-General as a necessary evil by which he could get approval for new taxes, the members of the Third Estate saw it as a national referendum. This was, they believed, their opportunity to create a new national government that would meet their needs. New ideas and old frustrations came to a head as the newly elected deputies of the Third Estate wended their way slowly to Versailles by coach, horse and foot in April 1789.

It was an assembly of many remarkable men, that included civil servants, businessmen, lawyers (the largest profession represented), priests, liberal nobles, scholars, soldiers and farmers. There were powerful leaders and leaders-to-be like the fiery Count de Mirabeau, the idealistic lawyer Maximilien Robespierre and the Abbé Sieyès. The abbé was that rare creature, a high clergyman whose sympathies lay

This engraving of the opening of the Estates-General shows some of the pomp and grandeur of Versailles, the king's country palace. Louis used this splendor as a tool to intimidate the deputies of the Third Estate. Note the king on the throne at the upper end of the hall. (The New York Public Library Picture Collection)

with the people. The peasants and workers, who were on society's lowest rung, had no representation at the Estates-General, although many middle-class deputies claimed to speak for them.

If the king professed to be the people's champion, he had no intention of letting them take control of the proceedings at Versailles. He did everything in his power to keep the Third Estate in its place. While the clergy of the First Estate arrived at the court in their traditional scarlet and purple vestments, and the nobles of the Second Estate in colorful silks and velvet capes, the members of the Third Estate were required to wear black. The aristocrats were granted a private audience with the king two days before the official opening of the assembly, but the people's deputies were kept waiting for hours for their royal audience. On May 4, the opening day itself, the Third Estate marched in the grand procession behind the court, nobles and clergy like some poor relation. The following day they were further humiliated when made to wait outside the assembly room while their "betters" were being seated.

No mention of reform was heard in Louis's first address to the Estates-General that afternoon. Instead he urged the deputies to be moderate in their discussions and expedient in approving the necessary taxes he needed to run the country. The king left it to his first minister, Jacques Necker, to threaten dismissal if the deputies decided to thwart the royal will.

But the humiliation of those first days at Versailles only fueled the anger and resolve of the Third Estate. They had waited 175 years for this opportunity to voice their concerns. If the king was going to ignore their needs, they would strike back by ignoring his. They elected Jean-Sylvain Bailly, an astronomer, as their president and then sat back and did nothing for five weeks.

During their strike, something remarkable happened. The "lower end" of the First Estate—the parish priests whose sympathies lay more with the poor than their ecclesiastical superiors— abandoned the clergies' meeting chamber and joined the Third Estate. But it was a high churchman, the Abbé Sieyès, who put forth a resolution calling for a "National Assembly of Representation of the French People." The resolution was overwhelmingly approved, and the members of the Third Estate, now the Assembly, were decreed "the only representatives legally and publicly recognized . . . by almost the entire nation." Taxes were not to be levied at the king's whim, but only by the Assembly, which represented the will of the people. It was a direct challenge to the king's power and came as a rude shock to the placid Louis. He quickly declared a Royal Session to be held on June 23 to deal with this insubordination, but didn't wait that long to retaliate.

On June 20, a dismal, rainy morning, the deputies of the Third Estate arrived at their meeting hall to find the doors locked and guarded by royal troops. When asked what the meaning of this was, the deputies were told that the hall was closed for "alterations." The people's representatives stood in the cold rain, uncertain what to do next. One deputy, the eminent Dr. Joseph Ignace Guillotin, suggested they repair to an indoor tennis court[1] in the neighborhood.

---

1. Tennis in the 18th century was a far more genteel sport than it is today. The French, who invented the game, called it *jeu de paume*, meaning "game of the palm," because players hit the ball back and forth over the net with the palm of their hand.

The royal court was a high-ceilinged hall with black walls to allow the white ball to be seen. In this unlikely setting, the Third Estate made its defiant stand against the king. President Bailly climbed up on the only table in the hall and tried to get the attention of the shouting deputies. After much yelling and debate, the members agreed to stay together until the constitution of the realm was firmly established.

"This proposition was greeted with loud acclaim, and several members of the assembly were moved to tears," wrote deputy Jacques-Antoine Creuzé-Latouche in his journal. "I saw several who joyfully took the heroic vow not to return home to wife and children until they had proved themselves more worthy of their loved ones by fulfilling their patriotic duty."

With the solemn Tennis Court Oath, the ball was now placed squarely in Louis XVI's court. If he had listened to the advice of Necker and met the people halfway, he might have remained in control of the situation. Instead he was swayed by the queen and reactionary relatives such as his brother, the Count d'Artois. They wanted Louis to stand firm and uphold his position as an absolute monarch. The king's speech on June 23 at the Royal Session was a vehement attack on the National Assembly and everything it stood for. He threatened to dismiss the Estates-General immediately if it did not return to the old order of business.

When the meeting ended, the king rose stiffly and left the hall, followed by the nobility and a good portion of the clergy. The members of the Third Estate stayed in their seats, as defiant as ever. After a time, the king's master of ceremonies returned and ordered them to leave the premises. Soldiers stood ready with bayonets to force them out. At this tense moment, the charismatic Count Mirabeau got to his feet and entered French history. "Tell your master that we are assembled here by the will of the people," Mirabeau said defiantly, "and that we will leave only at the point of a bayonet!"

It was the soldiers' cue to go into action. But they hesitated. How could they injure or kill other Frenchmen, including distinguished aristocrats and clergymen? So they did nothing. When news reached Louis of the Assembly's refusal to budge, he replied angrily, "Damn it, let them stay!" This first triumph for the people's representatives was a sweet one. Four days later the king ordered all remaining members of the first two estates to join the new National Assembly and work on drawing up a constitution for the nation. The Estates-General was no more. All this led one English observer, Arthur Young, to proclaim prematurely, "The whole business now seems over and the revolution complete."

The king may have capitulated to avoid bloodshed, but he was far from defeated. Since his own French troops were proving unreliable in this tense situation, Louis called up 25,000 Swiss and German mercenaries. He ordered them to surround Versailles and Paris in the event of a popular insurrection. At the same time a royalist plot was under way to replace Necker with an aristocrat, the Baron Louis de Breteuil, who would carry out the royal will more enthusiastically.

The people of Paris followed the events at Versailles with anxious fear. They believed the king's soldiers would descend on them at any moment. Wild rumors ran rampant through the narrow, twisting streets of the city. The fever reached its peak on July 11, when the king dismissed Necker. The people felt, and justly so, that they had lost their last friend at court.

July 14 promised to be another hot, humid day in the sweltering Parisian summer of 1789. The intense heat only added to an extremely volatile situation. Peasants and workers, not about to stand idly by and be slaughtered by the nearby troops, armed themselves with pitchforks, pikes and homemade spears. But these would provide scant defense against the muskets of the well-trained mercenaries. The people of Paris needed guns of their own to defend themselves, and they set off to find them.

A mob marched on the arsenal at the Invalides, an old military hospital. There the peasants and workers seized 30,000 muskets, but they still needed gunpowder to fire them. The word spread that the city's gunpowder supply was being stored at the ancient prison on the east end of the city—the Bastille. Like an army of angry ants, the mob swept through the street toward the fortress.

With its 100-foot-high stone walls and eight rounded towers, the Bastille rose above the squalid, working-class neighborhood of Saint-Antoine like a grim colossus of another age. Few buildings in Paris better symbolized the old regime and its cruel repressions than this 400-year-old walled fortress. In the past, it had held some of France's most distinguished prisoners including Diderot, Voltaire and that notorious profligate and erotic author, the Marquis de Sade. Although the Bastille had fallen into disuse years before, there were rumors that hundreds of prisoners still languished in its dank dungeons.

But if there was hatred in the hearts of the mob that stood before the Bastille that fateful morning, there was no burning desire to storm the fortress. The people wanted the gunpowder inside the Bastille and nothing more. This thought hardly comforted the prison's governor, Bernard de Launay. An excitable, nervous man of limited abilities, Launay was poorly equipped to deal with the crisis he now faced. When three delegates from the newly elected city government came into the Bastille under a flag of truce, he did his best to appear firm yet cordial. The governor refused to turn over the gunpowder and graciously insisted the delegates stay for lunch. If this was a delaying tactic, it only infuriated the impatient mob waiting outside.

By early afternoon another delegate, Thuriot de la Rozière, was allowed to enter the fort. Rozière chastized the other delegates for eating at the governor's table while the people of Paris went hungry in the streets. He told Launay that only if he surrendered the gunpowder now could he and his men expect mercy.

The governor knew he was in a poor position to hold out against the mob. He had only 110 men under his command, many of them old soldiers from the Invalides. Because the outer area of the Bastille was too large for them to defend, the governor and his small force had withdrawn earlier into the inner courtyard where a 75-foot moat and mounted cannon were all that protected them from the mob. While Launay wrestled with what to do next, two men from the crowd scaled the walls and hacked through the chains of the fort's outer drawbridge. The drawbridge came down with a crash and hundreds of people poured into the courtyard.

At the sight of the approaching mob, the defenders panicked, and without orders from Launay, began firing the cannon. The besiegers within were trapped. Scores dropped, dead; hundreds were wounded. Those still on their feet fired back, and a grim battle ensued.

Around 3 P.M. soldiers were sighted marching towards the prison. For a brief moment the governor took heart, believing them to be the king's troops come to rescue him. These soldiers, however, no longer

The storming of the Bastille signaled the start of the French Revolution. Although the fortress looks invincible in this drawing, it was undermanned and vulnerable. When the French Guards and their cannon arrived to join the siege, the Bastille's commander quickly surrendered. (The Bettmann Archives)

owed their allegiance to the king. They were the rebellious French Guards and the city militia who had joined forces to defend the city from nobles and foreigners. Even more disheartening for Launay, the soldiers were hauling their own cannon.

There was no point in continuing to fight, the governor decided. He had one of his men carry a note through an opened porthole in the

King Louis XVI (1754–1793)

Although he looks the model monarch in this portrait, Louis XVI was never happy being king. Upon hearing news that one of his ministers was quitting, Louis was heard to remark, "Why can't I resign too?" (The New York Public Library Picture Collection)

If Louis XVI had been born a locksmith or a huntsman, he might well have lived a happy and contented life. But fate made him king of France, and therein lies his tragedy.

As a youth in the decadent court of his grandfather, Louis XV, Louis cut a poor figure. Awkward, ill-at-ease socially and far from handsome, Louis was married off to the lively princess Marie-Antoinette of Austria when he was 16. He ascended the throne four years later, determined to win the love of his subjects.

inner drawbridge. A young bookkeeper in the crowd bravely crossed a plank dropped over the moat waters and grabbed the note. It read:

> We have more than twenty tons of gunpowder, and we will blow up the fortress and the whole neighborhood unless you allow us to surrender.

The commander of the French Guards accepted Launay's surrender. The defenders lowered the drawbridge, and the besiegers swarmed in. In one moment the Bastille fell, a symbol of centuries of royal oppression. But the mob had long forgotten the purpose of its

Louis was a weak leader with good intentions. He brought in new ministers to his court who would initiate long-needed reforms for France. But to take hold, reforms need a strong commitment. Louis was not the man for the job. He could not stand up to his nobles, who refused to sacrifice their own privileges and money to refill the national treasury. Louis couldn't even stand up to his queen, Marie-Antoinette, whose extravagance and bad advice contributed to his downfall.

The death of his elder son from tuberculosis in June 1789 was a personal blow that affected Louis's judgment at the critical time when the Estates-General was meeting. Under siege from the Third Estate, Louis lacked the ruthlessness to crush the Revolution in its infancy. He also lacked the foresight to go along with the plan for a constitutional monarchy that would allow him to remain king in a new France. Instead, he wasted precious time in fruitless plotting with foreign governments while giving lip service to the new government and its constitution.

Louis was neither the evil monster the revolutionaries made him out to be nor the saintly monarch the royalists mourned. He was a man of average abilities in a time that needed an extraordinary leader. History may judge his reign harshly, but one must have some sympathy for the man, for Louis XVI was as much a victim of the Revolution as he was its villain.

mission. They wanted revenge for their fallen comrades lying in the courtyard. They smashed furniture and destroyed whatever they could lay their hands on. The French Guards did what they could to control the bloodletting, but some of the Bastille's defenders could not be saved. Three men were hanged from a lamppost, and three others were cut down with swords and pikes.

Launay himself was marched under heavy guard through the street toward the City Hall. The hapless governor was stabbed, pelted with stones and had his hair torn from his head. At the very steps of City Hall and moments from safety, Launay seemed to give up all hope and, in despair, kicked a pastry cook in the groin. The mob descended on him with knives, bayonets and pistols. The vengeful cook cut through the dead man's neck with a knife. Launay's severed head was mounted on a pitchfork and paraded through the streets—a grisly trophy of the day.

Later that evening, as almost an afterthought, the dungeons of the Bastille were flung open. Inside, the liberators found four convicted forgers, two madmen and an aristocrat, jailed for immorality at the request of his own father. One of the lunatics had a long, white beard and thought he was Julius Caesar. He was paraded through the streets as a symbol of the regime's injustice and later carted off with his fellow madman to an asylum.

The Bastille was eventually torn down, stone by stone. Models made from the rubble were displayed and sold across Revolutionary France. As historian Simon Schama has perceptively noted, "The Bastille, then, was much more important in its 'afterlife' than it ever had been as a working institution of state. It gave a shape and an image to all the vices against which the Revolution defined itself."

It is no wonder that the start of the French Revolution is remembered to this day, not by the opening of the Estates-General or the Tennis Court Oath and its aftermath, but by the storming of the Bastille. The equivalent of the Fourth of July in the United States, Bastille Day, July 14, is now a national holiday in France.

CHAPTER 2 NOTES

p. 9   "What is it . . ." Richard Cobb and Colin Jones. *Voices of the French Revolution*, p. 26.

p. 12   "This proposition was greeted with loud acclaim . . ." Cobb and Jones, *Voices of the French Revolution*, p. 56.

p. 12   "Tell your master . . ." David Dowd, *The French Revolution*, p. 25.

p. 13   "The whole business now seems over . . ." Cobb and Jones, *Voices of the French Revolution*, p. 67.

p. 16   "We have more than twenty tons . . ." Dowd, *The French Revolution*, p. 39.

p. 18   "The Bastille, then, was much more important . . ." Simon Schama, *Citizens: A Chronicle of the French Revolution*, p. 408.

THE FIRST REVOLUTION

"The government . . . must, above all, guarantee inalienable rights which belong to all men, such as personal liberty, property, security, the protection of honor and life, free expression of thought, and resistance to oppression."
— The Declaration of the Rights of Man and the Citizen

Following the fall of the Bastille and the loss of his capital, Louis XVI stood at a crossroads. He could stay and fight or he could flee abroad to safety. He decided to do neither. Instead, he dismissed his troops around the city and entered Paris on July 17, 1789. The people greeted their king with wild cheers. Despite their disappointment with him, the people still retained a childlike faith in Louis. If only he would remove himself from the vengeful plotting of the nobles and his wife, whom they referred to irreverently as the "Austrian Woman," he could still lead them forward to a new France.

No better proof of the people's faith in Louis could be found than the newly fashioned cockade—the Revolution's first symbol. This knot of ribbon worn on the hats of the revolutionaries was red and blue, the colors of Paris, but it also had a stripe of white, the royal color. For his part, Louis wanted to live up to the people's image of him, and his intentions, however muddle-headed, were basically good. If this was the start of a revolution, the king hoped that, by coming to Paris freely, he could control and limit it.

The king's arrival in Paris did have a calming influence on the city, but the countryside was aflame with violence. During July and August, what came to be called "La Grande Peur" (the Great Fear) swept across France's towns and villages. Peasants, who had risen up against local authorities, feared reprisals from the royalists and began destroying the evidence that could condemn them. Chateaux were attacked and burned, feudal records of dues were destroyed and some landowners were even murdered.

Widespread lawlessness frightened the new revolutionaries as much as the aristocrats. Order had to be restored for the process of meaningful change to continue. The Assembly turned to the Marquis de Lafayette, the military hero who fought in the American Revolution, to help save their own. Lafayette was appointed commander of the new National Guard and given the job of putting down both royalist plots and peasant insurrections. Jean Sylvain Bailly, former president of the Assembly, was appointed mayor of Paris. Municipal councils were established in cities and towns throughout the nation to replace the king's councils.

On the evening of August 4, the Assembly met for a historic—and somewhat hysterical—session. In a flood of harangues, the deputies responded sympathetically to the peasant riots by pulling down the centuries-old foundations of feudal privilege. Lafayette's brother-in-law, the Viscount Louis-Marie de Noailles, proposed the abolition of feudal rights and, with it, much of the Second Estate's power. Still wanting to uphold the principle of private property, however, the deputies made provisions for financial compensation to landowners for their losses. The Assembly gained the trust of the people with these measures, and the violence and disorder subsided.

Now the deputies were ready to start work on what would become France's own declaration of independence, the Declaration of the Rights of Man and the Citizen. This document declared that "men are born and remain free and equal in rights." But it was a more philosophical document than the American Declaration of Independence, fuzzier and less specific. It not only was a declaration of the aims and purposes of the French Revolution, but was a call to arms to other nations to throw off their chains and march to liberty. As such, the Rights of Man was seen as a threat to every crowned head of Europe and planted seeds of international discord that would eventually ripen into war.

As important as the Rights of Man was a second decree several weeks later that forced the king to share his power with a legislative (the Assembly) and a judicial branch (the courts). The king could veto Laws made by the Assembly for as long as four years, but he could not dismiss them.

And what did Louis think of all this? He did not like it one bit, but he bided his time. Supported by the nobles and foreign friends, such as his wife's brother, the Emperor Leopold II of Austria, Louis felt confident he could still overturn the Assembly. In the meantime, he pretended to go along with the changes, so as not to arouse the Assembly's suspicions. If instead he had used this critical time to forge a new and meaningful alliance with the Revolutionary leaders, he might have saved his monarchy.

The king's true feelings came out in an unfortunate incident at Versailles. On October 1 the officers of one royal regiment were invited to dinner at the palace. In an enthusiastic display of loyalty to their king, the officers tossed the Revolutionary tricolored cockade to the floor and stepped on it. Louis looked on approvingly. News of the blasphemous gesture spread and incensed the people of Paris. They saw themselves being figuratively ground into the dust by the insensitive king and his nobles. Food shortages were seen not as a result of natural conditions and a weak political state, but as a royalist conspiracy. Although the people still held Louis in esteem, they felt that he had to be rescued from the poisonous influence of the court. This time the people didn't wait for him to come to them.

On October 5 a mob of angry women marched on City Hall, where they seized muskets and money. Then they started off on the road to Versailles. Their purpose was to speak to the king in person to find out why there wasn't enough bread to feed their hungry children. Like a storm gathering power as it crosses the sky, the marchers picked up new recruits at every step of the way. Lafayette, who could have used

Women played an active role in the Revolution. Here the women of Paris are shown marching to Versailles to confront the king over food shortages in October 1789. Note the well-to-do lady on the far left who seems to be pulled along by her sisters-in-arms almost against her will. (The Bettmann Archive)

the National Guard to stop the two-day march, hesitated. An astute politician, he realized that to thwart these women would make him as unpopular with the people as any royalist.

An autumn rainstorm didn't dampen the ardor of the women of Paris, who by nightfall were joined by many of their husbands. The angry crowd arrived at Versailles late the following afternoon. The Assembly, a political free-for-all at the best of times, was turned completely upside down by their arrival. The bedraggled women hung their wet stockings to dry from the public galleries and told off any speaker they didn't like in down-to-earth language. A small delegation of women was allowed to deliver their petition to the king. He pledged to have grain delivered to Paris for more bread, but this didn't satisfy the petitioners. They wanted the king himself to return to Paris with them, as a confirmation of his good faith. Lafayette persuaded Louis to make the journey under his safe escort the next day.

During the night, a small band of women burst into the palace, intent on murdering the queen in her bed. Two brave bodyguards gave their lives for their queen, allowing Marie-Antoinette to flee to her husband's room. Lafayette intervened in time to prevent further bloodshed, and the shaken royal couple appeared on the balcony to pacify the mob below.

The royal family, accompanied by the mob, began its journey to Paris at noon on October 6. The people's attitude toward their monarch was an odd mixture of respect and sarcasm. They called the king, the queen, and the dauphin, their son, "the baker, the baker's wife and the baker's boy." They sincerely hoped that the baker would provide the bread they so desperately needed.

The King took up residence at the Tuileries Palace in Paris, where he was joined two weeks later by the Assembly. The laws of the new France would no longer be made at the royal court; now they would be hammered out in the heart of Paris—the people's city. This was too much for 300 royal deputies, who resigned from the Assembly. Many of them fled abroad, hoping the king would follow their lead.

The departure of the monarchists seriously altered the balance of power in the National Assembly. Three main groups now sat in the new Assembly Hall, once the royal riding school. The moderates, the largest group, sat in the center of the hall with the president. Led by Lafayette, they sought a constitutional monarchy for France, patterned after the English system of government. The more radical revolutionaries, who wanted a truly democratic republic, sat to the left of the president. The royalists, now the smallest group, desired a return to the old ways before the Revolution. They sat to the right of the president. Liberals and conservatives have been positioned to the "left" or "right" ever since.

The Assembly Hall was not the only seat of political power in Paris. Political organizations, called "clubs," sprang up like mushrooms all over the city. The original purpose of these clubs was to discuss and debate ideas, but they gradually took on a more significant role in politics. While there were political clubs for royalists and moderates, such as Lafayette's "Club of 1789," the ones that rose to greatest prominence were the radical clubs. One of the most intellectual and well run of these was the Society of the Friends of the Constitution. Because they met in the old Convent of Saint-Jacques, they came to be called the Jacobin Club. Lawyer Robespierre from Arras was one of their most articulate and prominent members.

The Jacobins were largely middle class in outlook, but the Society of the Friends of the People, shortened to the Cordeliers after the name of the convent they met in, purported to represent the interests of the working classes. Their outspoken leader was another lawyer, Georges Jacques Danton from Arcis-sur-Aube. Danton had an ugly face but a golden tongue and was earning a reputation as a spellbinding speaker.

It is ironically fitting that the Jacobins and the Cordeliers should have made their headquarters in former religious convents. Institutionalized religion, like the monarchy, would be changed forever by the Revolution. The National Assembly, plagued by the same money problems that had faced the king and his ministers two years earlier, turned to the richest source of revenue in France, the Roman Catholic Church.

It was the worldly Charles Maurice de Talleyrand, bishop of Autun, who proposed that the church's vast land holdings be taken over by the government and sold to raise money. In July 1790 it was decreed that all priests and bishops should be elected by the people and required to swear an oath to the new French nation. Any clergyman who refused to take the oath would be dismissed.

This decree was a serious blunder on the part of the legislators. Although the high church in France was hopelessly corrupt, the people, particularly in the provinces, were devoutly religious. To them, the secularization of the church was akin to heresy. Thousands of clergymen refused to knuckle under to the new government and became heroes in the eyes of their parishioners, while the "constitutional" priests were branded as betrayers of the faith. In one reckless moment, the National Assembly had turned a revolution into a civil war. The legislators divided not only the church against itself, but the nation as well.

A second grave error was the Assembly's willingness to give the local municipal governments overriding power. Unlike the new United States of America, France forged a government too weak to unite the country under a central authority. Taxes could be levied on land, but if peasants didn't choose to pay them, no agency could make them pay. Even worse, the growing numbers of counterrevolutionaries—royalists, faithful Catholics and dissenting peasants—were free to organize their own fight against the forces of change.

In the face of these mounting problems, the moderates, led by Lafayette, saw that time was running out. If a constitutional monarchy was to be established, the Revolution had to be brought to an abrupt halt. The central player in this new government was about to frustrate their plans further. Louis, despite his complacent front, was ready to join the swelling ranks of émigrés and fight for his throne from outside France. The Count de Mirabeau, a leader of the Assembly, secretly urged the king to flee and appeal to the people from foreign soil. With the people's support, Louis could then overthrow the Assembly and establish a new one. The new body would be under the king's power, who would ultimately be under Mirabeau's control. The queen, however, detested Mirabeau as much as she distrusted Lafayette. After Mirabeau's death in April 1791, Marie-Antoinette, with the help of a sympathetic Swedish count, Hans Axel Fersen, devised a daring plan of escape.

The royal family would be disguised as the retinue of the Baroness de Korff, a German noblewoman, and flee by coach under cover of darkness to a town near the Austrian Netherlands border in northeast France.[1] The Marquis de Bouillé, a royalist general, would help Louis flee across the border with the promised assistance of loyalist French troops and the Austrian army. Once in Austrian territory, Louis could, with the help of his brother-in-law Leopold, lead a successful assault on the revolutionaries and retake France. It was a carefully thought out plan and one that began to unravel almost from the start.

On the evening of Monday, June 21, 1791—the longest day of the year—Count Fersen, disguised as a coachman, picked up the children—Mme Royale and Louis-Charles—and their governess, who was to impersonate Baroness de Korff. To avoid arousing suspicion, Fersen drove their hack around the city and returned later to get the others. The king's sister Madame Elisabeth, was disguised as a maid, and the king himself, as a manservant. The queen got lost in the dark and the flight was delayed as they waited anxiously for her.

At midnight, the royal family transferred to a large coach and were joined by three bodyguards. Fersen had wanted them to travel in two small coaches for speed, but Louis refused to break up the family. The

---

1. This part of the Netherlands was occupied at the time by the Austrian empire.

passport the party carried for free passage out of France was signed by the king himself.

The following morning, two accidents with the team of horses slowed the coach's progress. The delay caused the Duke of Choiseul, who was waiting to escort the coach at the first stopping station, to lose his nerve and move out, away from a gathering crowd of suspicious townspeople. The coach arrived to find no escort. It went on to the next stopping place, where the party was not expected. The local people sensed something wrong, and an alarm was raised. The coach managed to safely leave St.-Menchould, but not before a keen-eyed posting station manager recognized Louis from his portrait on the national paper currency.

The coach arrived at a bridge before the small town of Varennes to find an unpleasant surprise. The posting manager, in pursuit on horseback, had alerted the town's mayor, and the local National Guard had blocked the bridge with some overturned carts. The coach halted. It looked like the end of the road.

The family, refusing to identify themselves and sticking to their story, were taken to a local home for the night. At midnight, a justice of the peace from Versailles entered the house, saw the drably dressed "manservant" and fell to his knees. "Eh bien," sighed a resigned Louis, "I am indeed your King."

This contemporary propaganda sheet, called a broadside, shows the king's arrest at Varennes and the end of his flight from Paris. If Louis had agreed to have his family travel in two smaller coaches as a friend advised, he might have succeeded in escaping to Austria and history might have been very different. (The New York Public Library Picture Collection)

At 8 o'clock the next morning, the royal coach began the long journey back to Paris, escorted by thousands of people and three deputies from the Assembly. The journey that took one day out took four days back.

On the evening of June 25, the royal family arrived in Paris. The Assembly posted a sign along the route that showed its ambivalent feelings toward the wayward monarch. It read: "Anyone who applauds the king will be beaten, anyone who insults him will be hanged." One radical newspaper gave this report of the solemn procession:

> . . . the queen appeared upset and pretended to weep; the king, according to the account of the National Guards who spoke to the citizens lining the way, had got drunk at Pontin. This was no triumphal procession, it was the prison convoy of the monarchy!

The flight to Varennes couldn't have come at a worse time for the moderates. The Assembly was finishing work on the all-important constitution, and the king's actions put the whole process in jeopardy. But the legislators would not be thwarted. A constitutional monarchy without a monarch was nothing, so Louis was merely reprimanded for running away. He would be reinstated king, once he had signed and accepted the new constitution.

If the king's flight weakened Lafayette's position, it gave new strength to the Jacobins and Cordeliers, who hadn't trusted Louis from the start. While they still lacked the power to depose the king and establish a republic, their ideas were no longer whispered behind closed doors but now stated boldly in the Assembly Hall for all to hear.

The Cordeliers, the voice of the people, planned a public rally on July 17, 1791, three days after the second anniversary celebration of the fall of the Bastille. Members of the club placed a petition calling for the king's dismissal on the altar of the fatherland, erected specially for the Bastille celebration. Thousands of people turned out on the Champ de Mars, a parade ground, to sign the petition. Mayor Bailly, fearing a riot, ordered Lafayette's National Guard to break up the crowd. The once-hailed hero of France was jeered by the people. When someone fired a pistol in his direction, Lafayette gave his men the order to fire. When the smoke cleared, 13 people lay dead in the grass. By

Count de Mirabeau
(1749-1791)

Of all the early revolutionary leaders, none was more controversial than Honoré Gabriel Riqueti, better known as the Comte (Count) de Mirabeau. Mirabeau was a leading figure during the turbulent days of the Estates-General and the first National Assembly. If his bad habits and personal ambitions hadn't gotten the better of him, he might have changed the course of the revolution.

From the beginning, Mirabeau was the black sheep in a family of genteel nobility. He was jailed for misconduct as a young calvary officer and, after leaving the army as a captain, was arrested for debt in 1774. A lover of women and the good life, his scandalous behavior led

Mirabeau loved life and all its pleasures. Earlier in his career, he had abandoned a rich wife after spending her fortune. Such scandalous behavior shocked the king, who never fully trusted his cunning advisor. (The New York Public Library Picture Collection)

the end of the day, nearly another 40 people had died and many more were arrested. The "massacre of the Champ de Mars" drove another wedge into the unity of the revolutionaries. The common people of Paris and the moderate middle-class members of the Assembly were no longer united. They would never trust one another completely again.

to a two-year prison term. He later fled to the Netherlands and then England. Mirabeau greatly admired the British system of government with its constitutional monarchy, free press and Parliament. He returned to France a committed liberal.

After being rejected as a deputy for the Second Estate, he was elected to the Third Estate from Aix in the Estates-General. Although physically repulsive with bulging eyes and a face scarred by smallpox, Mirabeau was an electrifying speaker and an eloquent writer. His courageous stand before the king's representative at Versailles earned him the title the "Tribune of the People." In 1791 he was elected president of the National Assembly.

Mirabeau worked feverishly as the liaison between the king and the Assembly, hoping to save the Revolution from anarchy and to establish a constitutional monarchy. He tried to manipulate the king to gain personal power for himself, but Louis detested Mirabeau's immoral lifestyle and the queen despised his liberal leanings.

In April 1791, overworked and overindulged, Mirabeau died of exhaustion at age 42. His last words were "I carry with me the ruin of the monarchy." He spoke the truth. A year later his secret negotiations to restore the king to power were uncovered, and soon after Louis was brought to trial for treason. The remains of the "Tribune of the People" were removed from the Pantheon, where France's greatest heroes were interred, and thrown into a common grave. Thus did the Revolution deal with those who betrayed it.

As for Lafayette, he had fallen from his pedestal. The man who dreamed of saving France now could not save his reputation. He was dismissed from his command. Other leaders of the Revolution dropped out of sight as martial law was declared. Robespierre changed his address. Danton fled to England. And Jean-Paul Marat, a fiery journalist gaining a reputation as a defender of the people, literally went underground and took up residence in the vast Parisian sewer system. The gases and filth there gave Marat a horrible skin disease that would plague him for the rest of his life.

Gradually order returned and the Assembly finished its work on the constitution. On September 14 Louis XVI swore to uphold the new law of the land and was reinstated king. As September drew to a close, the first National Assembly, its work done, dissolved itself. Elections were held for a new legislative body as dictated by the constitution.

One enlightened nobleman, the Marquis de Ferrières, wrote to his wife on this historic occasion:

> The king and queen . . . appear entirely in favor of the constitution, and they are wise to be so. I hope that all interests will be reconciled, but we must see the new legislature. . . .The people are delirious. The king and queen are acclaimed the moment they appear; so you see, everything points to a solid new order of affairs.

The Revolution, it seemed to many, was over. A new French nation looked forward to a bright and shining future. But it would soon become apparent that this "solid new order" was built on a foundation of sand.

CHAPTER 3 NOTES

p. 19 "The government . . . must, above all . . ." Richard Cobb and Colin Jones, *Voices of the French Revolution*, p. 81.

p. 26 "*Eh bien* . . ." Simon Schama, *Citizens: A Chronicle of the French Revolution*, p. 554.

p. 27 "Anyone who applauds the king . . ." Schama, *Citizens*, p. 558.

p. 27 ". . . the queen appeared upset . . ." Cobb and Jones, *Voices of the French Revolution*, p. 121.

p. 30 "The king and queen . . ." Cobb and Jones, *Voices of the French Revolution*, p. 124.

THE NATION
GOES TO WAR

"War is actually a national benefit . . . a people . . . needs war to banish from its bosom the men who might corrupt liberty."
— Jacques Pierre Brissot

The new Legislative Assembly that convened on October 1, 1791 faced a plethora of problems. Inflation and a scarcity of food were the most serious. Food shortages had been a problem in France for years, but with hoarding and rising prices, the situation was steadily worsening.

With Lafayette's star fading, Mirabeau dead, and the King effectively stripped of all power, a new group of leaders came to the fore. This group was comprised of middle-class liberals with high ideals and a gift for oratory. Their leader was Jacques Brissot, a brilliant and widely traveled journalist. He and two other leading speakers of the group came from the Bordeaux region in southern France, near the River Gironde, and came to be called Girondists.

If the Jacobins were radical democrats, the Girondists were moderate liberals. Their centrality gave them their strength in the new

Legislative Assembly. But the Girondists had one serious flaw in their collective character. For all their ideals, they lacked the fortitude to turn those ideals into meaningful action. The Girondists were dreamers in a time of crisis that cried out for doers.

Unlike the Jacobins, they were less a political club than an intimate circle of friends. One of Brissot's closest friends was a colorless civil servant called Jean-Marie Roland. Roland's wife, Madame Roland, was a strong-willed, ambitious woman with a charismatic personality. A strange cross between Lady Liberty and Marie-Antoinette, she would become a central figure among the Girondists.

Many a government beset by domestic troubles has gone to war to divert the people's attention from empty stomachs and purses. The Girondists were no different. With an array of thorny problems before them, they seized on the most tangible one—the Revolution's enemies abroad. The danger of foreign invasion was hardly imaginary. Thousands of émigrés, mostly aristocrats and monarchists, were forming an army with the help of Austria and Prussia. They planned to cross the Rhine River and retake France from the revolutionaries. A greater threat to France than the émigrés, however, were the Austrians and Prussians, who wanted to crush the Revolution and take control of the country for themselves.

The king approved of the Girondist plan of war, although he was secretly hoping Austria would win and restore him to power. Lafayette supported the effort, hoping victory on the battlefield would add luster to his tarnished reputation. As for the people, they largely believed that a declaration of war would unite their troubled country and spread the ideals of freedom abroad in a way no revolution ever had done before.

The only ones opposed to war were Robespierre and the Jacobins. They advocated the establishment of a republic and saw the war cries as a diversionary tactic that the Girondists and the king were using for their own ends. For the Jacobins, the real enemies were the counterrevolutionaries within France. Until they were weeded out, the nation could not be secure. But the Jacobins' dissent was drowned out by the voice of the majority.

In January 1792 the Assembly sent an ultimatum to Emperor Leopold of Austria and Frederick Wilhelm of Prussia. The Assembly told them to renounce war and declare their friendship with France. In

The sheet music of "La Marseillaise" features French soldiers going off to fight the Prussians, for whom the song was first written. In 1992 a movement to change the French national anthem's lyrics was led by the wife of President François Mitterrand. Critics complained that the song's bloodthirsty words were out of step with our more "peaceful" world. (The New York Public Library Picture Collection)

March two developments occurred that made war all but inevitable. Leopold died and his hot-tempered son ascended the Austrian throne. Soon after Louis dismissed his war minister, the Count of Narbonne, and appointed several leading Girondists to the cabinet. Jean-Marie Roland became minister of justice and Charles François Dumouriez, minister of foreign affairs. Dumouriez was that rarity among Girondists—a leader who backed words with action.

On April 20 the king made a formal declaration of war against Austria before the Assembly. The plan, as devised by Dumouriez, was simple. The Revolutionary army would strike north with lightning speed in Belgium, under Austrian control since 1713, and surprise the enemy. The same dissension, however, that had divided the rich and the poor across the country worked to divide officers and common soldiers in the army. As a result, the attack was a complete and utter disaster. Soldiers would not take orders from their officers, who often didn't know how to handle them. Demoralized troops broke ranks under poor leadership. One general who ordered a hasty retreat was hanged by his own men for cowardly behavior. The Austrians and Prussians had a golden opportunity to counterattack and take over France, but amazingly, they didn't.

The Girondists took the blame for the failure of the campaign. The Jacobins, until now a minority in the Assembly, grew in strength as the opposition party. To retain power, the Girondists decided to move farther to the left to keep the Jacobins at bay. They ordered all nonjuring priests, those who had refused to take an oath of allegiance to the nation, to leave France. Next the Girondists dismissed the king's bodyguard, a stinging blow to Louis, who responded by dismissing more ministers. It was a time of angry recriminations, bitter accusations and mounting fear. Fortunately, Dumouriez kept his head, resigned from the ministry and went north personally to take command of the army.

Besides a new commander, the army also had a new anthem. Claude Joseph Rouget de Lisle, an army engineer and amateur composer, wrote the "War Song of the Army of the Rhine" for French soldiers going to fight the Prussians and Austrians. A regiment of 600 soldiers from the seaside city of Marseilles sang the stirring song as they marched toward Paris that summer to join the people in opposing the king. It soon became the favorite song of French soldiers as they defended their country from foreign invaders. By that time it had come to be called "La Marseillaise," after the gallant troops that had first brought it to national attention. "Nothing like the 'Marseillaise' has ever been written that comes so near to expressing the comradeship of citizens in arms and nothing ever will," Simon Schama has written.

The lyrics alone would support this opinion:

Arise you children of our motherland
Oh now is here our glorious day!
Over us the bloodstained banner
Of tyranny holds sway.
Oh, do you hear there in our fields
The roar of those fierce fighting men?
Who come right here into our midst
To slaughter sons, wives and kin.

To arms, O citizens
Form up in closed ranks
March on, march on!
And drench our fields
With their tainted blood.

One military leader later claimed "La Marseillaise" brought 100,000 new recruits into the French army. In 1795, the patriotic hymn became the official French national anthem.[1]

But neither war nor its songs could allay the frustrations and anger of the people of Paris. They continued to be shut out of the legislative process under the constitution and saw violence as the only means to express their will. They now called themselves *sans-culottes*, which literally means "without knee breeches." Unlike the French aristocrats, these common people did not wear fashionable knee-length breeches, but long trousers that identified them as working class. The name

---

1. In 1992, on the 200th anniversary of "La Marseillaise," a movement was under way headed by France's First Lady, Danielle Mitterrand, to revise the song's lyrics, making them less bloodthirsty. Most French people were opposed to this tampering with their national anthem.

sans-culottes soon came to describe any Revolutionary political activist. A radical pamphlet of the day gave this sharp definition of a sans-culottes:

> This is a creature who always goes on foot, who does not own millions . . . has no servants to do his bidding . . . He is useful, for he knows how to work in the fields, or in a smithy or sawmill, how to use a file, how to cover a roof, make his own clogs—and how to pour out his blood to the last drop for the good of the republic.

On June 20, 1792 a a large parade of sans-culottes celebrated the third anniversary of the Tennis Court Oath. The parade quickly turned into a riot. The mob, bearing pikes, invaded the Assembly Hall and presented a petition against the king to the deputies. The marchers then continued on to the Tuileries Palace. Although the mob was out for blood, Louis faced them with steely courage. The same monarch who read the newspaper and fell asleep in meetings with his ministers now proved there was still some majesty left in the Bourbon blood. Louis managed to save his life, but not his dignity. The sans-culottes insisted he don a *bonnet rouge*, the red stocking cap that was a symbol of the people, and drink a cup of wine to the nation's health. The invaders were appeased and left.

What was so frightening about the episode was not the king's helplessness but the helplessness of the legitimate government to do anything to stop it. The people were seizing control at last, and neither Girondists nor Jacobins wanted to arouse their rage.

Lafayette, like many moderates, had been passed over by the Revolution he had helped set in motion. The people hanged him in effigy. Even the king had no use for him any more. The marquis fled to the battlefront. There he tried to rally his troops to turn on Paris, but his words were ignored. Rejected by his own soldiers, Lafayette fled to the border, was captured by the Austrians and spent the next five years as a prisoner of war.

With Lafayette gone, all hopes for a constitutional monarchy faded quickly. In July the Girondists, fearful of losing their grip on the government, called the National Guard to Paris as a defense against both the sans-culottes and the counterrevolutionaries. But like the army, the Guard was divided in its loyalties and could no longer be relied on to keep order.

On August 3 the sans-culottes gave the Assembly an ultimatum: either dethrone the king in six days, or the people would do it for them. The deadline drew closer, and the Assembly did nothing. On August 9 the sans-culottes organized their own "Insurrectionary Commune," a self-governing body of political activists.

The next day was hot and humid. The Assembly was nearly deserted. Four hundred deputies, fearful for their lives, stayed home. The new commander of the National Guard, who tried to stop a mob marching on the Tuileries Palace, was murdered. The Guard, now leaderless, was incapable of preventing further bloodshed. The mob marched on the palace. Louis knew that this mob would not be as easily appeased as the last one that visited him. The king reluctantly left the palace with his family for the relative safety of the Assembly Hall. As he crossed the well-manicured grounds, Louis was heard to mutter "The leaves are falling early this year."

The Swiss Guard, Louis's only remaining loyal soldiers, were left behind to defend the palace. By midmorning a battle was raging between the Swiss Guard and the invading mob. The king called for a cease-fire, thinking it would end the fighting. But what followed made the bloodshed at the Bastille seem mild. The sans-culottes fell on the retreating soldiers with a ferocious savagery. Six hundred or more of the Swiss Guard were cut down where they stood. The frenzy for blood was so fierce that some unfortunate rebels from Brest were murdered because their red uniforms were mistaken for those of the Swiss. Later the bodies were cruelly mutilated and limbs fed to the dogs.

The Assembly held its breath in horror. But, for the time being, the sans-culottes were content with bringing down the monarchy. They reasoned that the country might need the government if foreign invaders attacked. The Assembly, under pressure from the Commune, suspended the king from all power and had him and his family imprisoned in the dark and gloomy headquarters of the Knights Templar. There Louis awaited trial until after a new assembly was elected. In the meantime, the Commune ruled Paris. That radical body divided the city into 48 neighborhoods, or "sections." Bands of sans-culottes could be mobilized from each section at a moment's notice to march,

Jacques Louis David (1748–1825)

David was the most successful artist of the Revolutionary period. His career, however, did not get off to a good start. After losing the coveted Prix de Rome four times, David attempted suicide by starvation. He survived, won the prize on his fifth try and went to Rome to paint. There he came under the powerful influence of classical Roman art. (The Bettman Archive)

If the pen is mightier than the sword, then in the hand of an artist like David, the paintbrush may be the mightiest weapon of all. David raised propaganda to the level of high art in a series of epic paintings that have come to symbolize the ideals and passions of the French Revolution.

As a young artist, David traveled to Italy, where he found inspiration in the classical subjects of ancient Rome. His first great painting, *The Oath of the Horatii* (1785), used an episode from Roman history to express a militant patrio-

demonstrate and riot. The new assembly, the Commune made clear, would be elected by all citizens, regardless of their station, and it would execute their will.

In the third week of August a strange new invention was unveiled on the Place du Carrousel right across from the Tuileries. People stared and pointed at the odd contraption, which was called by many "the

tism that foreshadowed the Revolution in France. An idealist, David was fervently committed to the Revolution and became a deputy to the National Convention. In 1792 this former court painter voted for the death of his one-time patron, the king.

In his masterpieces, *The Tennis Court Oath* and *The Death of Marat*, David captured the high drama of Revolutionary France. His dying Marat is a blessed martyr, a far cry from the living firebrand. David painted the portrait from the corpse itself, which he had specially embalmed. Marat's fatal wound was carefully sewn shut and even his ugly skin condition was covered cosmetically to make him appear more saintly.

As the Revolution grew more radical, David took on the added role of festival director and theatrical designer. He staged elaborate parades and spectacular fetes to raise people's thoughts from the guillotine to the higher realm of republican idealism. David's talents even extended to fashion design, as he created appropriate dress for fashionable revolutionaries.

After the Jacobins' downfall in July 1794, David was imprisoned, but he escaped the guillotine and was later released. He soon found a second career in depicting the glorious achievements of France's new savior, the Emperor Napoléon. When Napoléon fell and the Bourbon monarchy was restored, David wisely left for Brussels. There he spent his last years painting sentimental portraits for wealthy patrons. A great artist, David was also an opportunist and one of the Revolution's few survivors.

machine." Its steely blade was said to be a humane improvement over the executioner's sword or the hangman's noose. It was the guillotine.

CHAPTER 4 NOTES

p. 31   "War is actually a national benefit . . ." N.S. Pratt, *The French Revolution*, p. 51.

p. 35   "Nothing like the 'Marseillaise' has ever . . ." Simon Schama. *Citizens: A Chronicle of the French Revolution*, p. 598.

p. 36   "This is a creature . . ." Richard Cobb and Colin Jones, *Voices of the French Revolution*, p. 190.

p. 37   "The leaves are falling . . ." Schama, *Citizens*, p. 614.

A SORT OF
JUSTICE

"I die innocent of all the crimes of which I have been
charged. I pardon those who have brought about my death
and I pray that the blood you are about to shed may never
be required of France . . ."
—last recorded words of Louis XVI

"The king is dead; long live the republic!"
—the crowd at Louis's execution

The National Assembly, under pressure from the
Commune, both extended democratic reform and limited it in the
summer of 1792. Laws were passed that gave the vote to every French-
man over 21 and opened army commissions on the basis of merit and
not by class or birth. Other laws, however, put the National Guard
under the control of the sans-culottes and allowed police to search
homes without warrants and arrest anyone suspected of being a counterrevolutionary.

The Girondists were still in power, but only by the will of the Paris
Commune. Roland and four other Girondists made up a temporary

Executive Council of ministers to replace the king. The sixth member of the Council and its leader, was Georges Jacques Danton, the man they now called the "Lord High Sans-culotte." No other political leader better expressed the dreams and desires of the people or had a stronger influence over the Commune.

Danton used this influence to bring the people's attention back to the enemies outside the closed gates of Paris. The war was going badly and new recruits were desperately needed. In perhaps the greatest speech of his career, Danton roused the people to action. "The tocsin [alarm bell] that we are going to sound is no alarm bell, it is the signal for the charge against the enemies of the fatherland," he proclaimed before the Assembly on September 2. "To vanquish them, gentlemen, we must show daring, more daring, and again daring; and France will be saved!"

Danton also darkly alluded to the "traitors within" who were a threat to the nation. Many of these enemies—priests, aristocrats and other counterrevolutionaries—were now in prison. But how long could they be kept there? Behind bars, these traitors mixed freely with the criminal classes and might win them to their cause. Rumors of an impending prison insurrection spread through Paris.

Mass hysteria was brought to a fever pitch on the same day as Danton's famous speech when the approaching Prussian army took Verdun, the last buffer before Paris. "What then followed," writes Simon Schama, "has no equal in atrocities committed during the French Revolution by any party."

The afternoon of September 2, two dozen nonjuring priests were moved by coach across the city to the Abbaye prison. They were accompanied by a mob who were determined that the prisoners would never see the light of day again. One by one the terrified priests were interrogated by a specially appointed commissioner. This was merely a legal formality. After a few minutes of questioning, each condemned man was shoved down some steps into the prison garden, where his "executioners," armed with axes, knives, and swords, were waiting. In 90 minutes, 19 priests lay dead, hacked to pieces.

This slaughter merely whetted the mob's taste for blood. They moved on to the Carmes prison, formerly a Carmelite convent. Again, each prisoner was questioned, all were found guilty, and 150 more hapless priests were killed in their cells. Some priests chose a more merciful exit than the one awaiting them and threw themselves from the prison wall to instant death in the street.

As the slaughter mounted, the killers grew less selective in their victims. They marched on three more prisons and dragged out any prisoner they could find. The vast majority were common criminals and beggars innocent of any crime against the Revolution. Many were boys in their teens; some, mere children. For good measure, some of the mob returned to the Abbaye to kill 300 more prisoners.

The "September Massacres," as they came to be called, went on for five days. By its end, 1,400 people, about half of all the prisoners in Paris, were dead. Only about 400 of these were guilty of any crime against the Revolution.

The radical journalist Jean-Paul Marat, who had suggested that the priests be sent openly across the city, may have well been the main instigator for the massacres. But not one political leader in the city raised a hand to stop the carnage. Danton called the executions "an indispensable sacrifice," and Roland, minister of the interior, feebly claimed the slaughter represented "a sort of justice."

The September Massacres and the events leading up to them, changed the very nature of the Revolution, moving it irrevocably to the left. On September 21, the newly elected National Convention met for the first time, abolished the monarchy and proclaimed France a republic. In October Danton resigned from the Executive Council and shifted his alliance from the Girondists to Robespierre.

Now there were only two principal points of view concerning France's future: the Girondists on the right and the Jacobins on the left. In the Convention, the Jacobins and more extreme radicals sat toward the back of the hall on high benches. Hence they came to be called "the Mountain." Between the Mountain and the Girondists, the mass of uncommitted deputies formed the "marsh" or "plain." The two central forces of the National Convention swayed these uncommitted members back and forth in an unending power play.

While the Mountain was steadily growing in strength, the Girondists managed to hold on to their power, thanks mostly to Dumouriez's skillful handling of the war and the provinces' negative reaction to the atrocities committed in Paris. Dumouriez's triumph at Valmy on Sep-

20 over the Prussians was a decisive victory. The general
Brussels, the capital of Belgium, in December 1792 as a
co.. ering hero.

The Girondists, however, did not use their power wisely. Roland's attacks on Robespierre, the Mountain's leader, were shrill and personal. They gained Robespierre more sympathizers than enemies. Furthermore, the Girondists, unlike the Mountain, did not have a strong political base among the people. They spent their energies bickering among themselves and their enemies and neglected to make strong connections with the masses and plan their political future. The Girondists' proposal for a federation of self-governing districts held little appeal for the Commune. The Commune found Robespierre's call for a strong central government in Paris far more attractive because it would give its members more power.

Amid this power struggle there remained the lingering question: What should be done with the king? One answer was given on the Convention floor by a 25-year-old intellectual and poet named Louis Antoine Léon de Saint-Just. The youngest deputy there, Saint-Just idolized Robespierre. With his long black hair and innocent good looks, Saint-Just resembled nothing so much as an angel. His efforts in the Mountain's behalf would soon earn him the nickname "The Angel of Death." In a spellbinding speech, Saint-Just called for the king's death as a necessary sacrifice to allow the new republic to live. The speech was well received, but another event that occurred shortly before it was what really set the stage for the king's demise.

A locksmith had discovered an iron chest in the king's quarters in the Tuileries Palace. Inside the chest were incriminating papers going back several years. They revealed the king's antirevolutionary feelings, secret plots, and plans for the flight to Varennes. Also incriminated were Louis's correspondents, including Lafayette and Mirabeau. The chest was first opened by the Girondists, who were accused of altering evidence to protect the king. Although the evidence was inconclusive, it further damaged Louis's tarnished image. He was labeled an "enemy of the Revolution," and the Girondists had no choice but to put him on trial.

On December 11 the accused, referred to in the records not as Louis XVI but "Louis Capet," was brought from the Temple prison to the Convention for trial. In the three hours he was questioned, Louis

The execution of Louis XVI on January 21, 1792 was a turning point in the Revolution. As the executioner held up the king's head, the people cried, "The king is dead; long live the republic!" (The New York Public Library Picture Collection)

retained a regal dignity, although his lapses in memory were not convincing. Only once, when accused of shedding his countrymen's blood through his devious acts, did he grow emotional. "No, sir!" Louis cried, rising to his feet. "I did not do that." Nevertheless, he was indicted on 33 counts.

The defense began its case on the day after Christmas. Its central argument was that the Convention was not a judicial body and didn't

Joseph Ignace Guillotin (1738–1814) and the Guillotine

Despite the stern expression he wears on this bust, Dr. Guillotin was a humane and kind man. The machine that now bears his name would, he felt, make executions both painless and democratic. (The New York Public Library Picture Collection)

"The hot hand." "The widow." "The national razor." "The blade of the law." These are all euphemisms for one of the most infamous instruments of execution ever devised by man—the guillotine. Because of its blood-curdling reputation, people seldom remember that the guillotine was once considered a merciful alternative to far crueller means of execution.

Joseph Ignace Guillotin was a well-respected Parisian doctor and a deputy of the National Assembly who in December 1789 first proposed to the nation a means of painless, mechanical decapitation. Guillotin saw such a machine as being humanitarian as well as democratic. For centuries, beheading was reserved for the nobility, while common criminals were subjected to a number of more grisly deaths, from burning to being torn apart

have the right to try the king. Since the people had given the Convention absolute powers, this argument was brushed aside. The Girondists were growing nervous. They realized that if the king were to die, their own fate would be sealed. Therefore, they proposed that the French

by horses. Guillotin proposed that all the condemned, whatever their class, be executed by his machine. "The mechanism falls like thunder;" he explained, "the head flies off, blood spurts, the man is no more."

His proposal, however, stalled for two years in Assembly debate. Disillusioned, the good doctor abandoned his idea, but a surgeon, Dr. Louis, took it up with professional enthusiasm. Louis hired a German piano maker to build a prototype of Guillotin's machine to his own specifications. The surgeon's design called for "two uprights, a foot apart, with grooves down which ran a well-tempered blade, heavy enough to fall rapidly and give a decided blow to the victim, who is to be lying flat on his stomach with his head across a block of wood immediately below the blade."

Guillotin's machine was finally adopted as France's official instrument of execution in the spring of 1792. On April 25 Nicholas Pelletier, a thief and forger, had the dubious honor of being the first human to face this new "dignified death." Thousands more would follow in his footsteps before the Revolution ended—2,690 in Paris alone during the Reign of Terror.

The machine was at first called the "Louison" or "Louisette" after the surgeon who perfected it, but credit was soon given to its originator. Ironically, Dr. Guillotin came to resent his name being associated with an instrument whose reputation quickly lost its humanitarian luster.

The guillotine's work did not end with the Revolution that gave it birth. It remained the official means of execution in France until September 1977, when a Tunisian immigrant and murderer became the last person to stand before "the blade of the law." Four years later capital punishment was abolished in France.

people decide on a verdict in a national vote. Robespierre argued that such a referendum could result in civil war. The matter was settled. Louis's fate would be decided by the deputies of the Convention. At Marat's insistence, the vote was held publicly. A large majority of the deputies found Louis guilty of treason. Only his sentence remained to be decided.

Throughout a bitterly cold January night, the deputies debated what the penalty would be. By dawn they had reached their decision: 361 voted for death; 319, for imprisonment and eventual banishment.

Louis XVI accepted his fate with a grace and strength that he had never displayed as a ruler. In the face of death, like many victims of the Revolution to come, he rose to the occasion. On January 20, a sad reunion took place at the Temple, where the king bid farewell to his family. To end their grief, Louis promised to see his wife and children once more in the morning before his execution. It was a promise he never intended to keep.

After confessing his sins to an Irish priest, Louis got a good night's sleep. He awoke early, heard mass in his room, and said good-bye to his faithful valet, who was more distressed than the king himself. At 8 A.M. Louis climbed into the coach for his last journey to the Place de la Revolution, which had once borne his grandfather's name. There 20,000 people had gathered to watch him go before the guillotine. The ride through the crowded, fog-filled streets took two hours.

At the foot of the scaffold, the king removed his coat and climbed the steps, refusing any assistance. The executioner tied Louis's hands and shaved his neck to make the blade's work easier. Like many of the condemned, Louis was given the opportunity to say a few last words. "My people," he began, addressing the massive crowd, "I die inno-cent . . ." The captain of the guard, wishing to avoid an incitement to riot, gave the signal for the drums to roll. Much of the rest of what Louis said was lost in the thundering tattoo. He was strapped down on the wooden plank, his head set in the fatal slot. The heavy, 12-inch blade dropped. The executioner lifted the dripping head from the basket and held it high for the public's view. "His blood flowed and cries of joy from eighty thousand armed men struck my ears . . ." wrote one en-tranced observer. "I saw people pass by, arm in arm, laughing, chatting familiarly as if they were at a fete."

What followed was described more sympathetically in a letter by the royalist Bernard to his mother: ". . . his body and head were immediately taken to the parish cemetery and thrown into a pit fifteen foot deep, where they were consumed by quicklime. And so there remains nothing of this unhappy prince except the memory of his virtues and of his misfortune."

The living symbol of the old regime was gone. What lay ahead was a brave, new world, both terrifying and exhilarating.

CHAPTER 5 NOTES

p. 41   "I die innocent . . ." Simon Schama, *Citizens: A Chronicle of the French Revolution*, p. 669.

p. 41   "The king is dead . . ." David Dowd, *The French Revolution*, p. 101.

p. 42   "The tocsin that we are going to sound . . ." Richard Cobb and Colin Jones, *Voices of the French Revolution*, p. 156.

p. 42   "What then followed . . ." Schama, *Citizens*, p. 631.

p. 47   "The mechanism falls . . ." Schama, *Citizens*, p. 621.

p. 47   "two uprights, a foot apart . . ." Cobb and Jones, *Voices of the French Revolution*, p. 97.

p. 48   "His blood flowed . . ." Schama, *Citizens*, p. 670.

p. 49   ". . . his body and head were immediately taken . . ." Cobb and Jones, *Voices of the French Revolution*, p. 174.

THE VIEW FROM ABROAD

"... the liberty of the whole earth was depending on the issue of the contest, and was ever such a prize won with so little innocent blood?"

—Thomas Jefferson

"Are these 'the Rights of Man'? Is this the LIBERTY of Human nature? The most savage four footed tyrants that range the unexplored deserts of Africa in point of tenderness, rise superior to these two-legged Parisian animals."

—*London Times*, September 10, 1792

The execution of Louis XVI sent shock waves throughout Europe and the United States. People everywhere reeled in horror at the killing of the French monarch. English Prime Minister William Pitt called it "the foulest and most atrocious act the world has ever seen." The revolutionaries were seen as inhuman, bloodthirsty beasts who would not stop until all of Europe was thrown into utter anarchy.

It had not always been so. When the Revolution began, many of France's friends and neighbors were sympathetic and supportive to-

The fear and hatred the Revolution inspired abroad comes through clearly in this bitter English cartoon. A sans-culotte fiddles merrily while the guillotine prepares to claim another victim. The caption that accompanies it reads: "The Zenith of French Glory; The Pinnacle of Liberty. Religion, Justice, Loyalty and all the Bugbears of Unenlightened Minds, Farewell!" (The Bettmann Archive)

ward the French people and their attempt to change their country. None were more supportive than the Americans. ". . . The attention of all . . . is fixed on the meeting of the Assembly of the Estates General," proclaimed Boston's *Massachusetts Magazine* in April 1789. "What advantage will result to the kingdom from this meeting, time only will determine. We may venture, however, as republicans, to predict that they will be salutary . . ."

When the Bastille fell, Lafayette sent the key of the infamous prison to the new American president and his old commander, George Washington. The letter that accompanied this symbol of tyranny claimed it was "a tribute which I owe . . . as a missionary of liberty to its patriarch."

This was no mere phrase-making on Lafayette's part. He and thousands of Frenchmen looked to the American Revolution as their model and inspiration. Some of them had fought side by side with the colonists against the British. Now the Americans could repay the debt by supporting the French Revolution.

In a letter to U.S. envoy Gouverneur Morris in Paris, Washington wrote in October 1789 "The revolution . . . in France is of so wonderful a nature, that the mind can hardly recognize the fact," and predicted "that nation will be the most powerful and happy in Europe . . ."

But Morris himself had his doubts. On becoming the American minister to France in 1792, Morris questioned both Lafayette's and Mirabeau's abilities to control events. In retrospect, this was a sound judgment. When the mob overran the Tuileries in August 1792, Morris helped save the lives of aristocrats seeking sanctuary, some of them veterans of the American Revolution. "I will not turn them out of it [his home] let what will happen to me," Morris told an American visitor. "They are all persons to whom our country is more or less indebted, and had they no such claim upon me, it would be inhuman to force them into the hands of the assassins."

As the Revolution turned more radical, many Americans came to share Morris's views. Even the stalwart Washington, in reaction to the violence in Paris, noted ominously that "the tumultuous populace of large cities are ever to be dreaded."

But long before the September Massacres, a critic arose in England who would become an eloquent spokesman for antirevolutionary feeling everywhere. British statesman Edmund Burke would at first glance appear ill cast in the role of antirevolutionary. As a member of Parliament and leader of the liberal Whig opposition, Burke had defended the rights of the American colonists during their Revolution. But for Burke, the French Revolution was less a freeing from tyranny than the building of a dangerous new order, without regard for individual freedoms or established institutions.

Like the Americans, the French forged a constitution to define the rights of its citizens. The constitution of 1793, presented in this allegoric picture by Robespierre, was the second of four constitutions to be produced by the Revolution. It was the most democratic of all the constitutions, but unfortunately was never fully implemented. (The New York Public Library Picture Collection)

Marquis de Lafayette
(1757–1834)

If any one person embodied the best hopes of the French Revolution to Americans, it was Marie Joseph Paul Yves Roch Gilbert du Motier, better known as the Marquis de Lafayette.

Lafayette was born into a family of great wealth and a long military tradition. His father died in battle when the boy was only two. The young Lafayette studied at the Military Academy in Versailles and became a captain in the cavalry. The life of a courtier in the court of Louis XVI did not interest the adventurous youth, so at 19 he bought a ship and sailed to America with a band of volunteers to join the colonies in their struggle against Great Britain.

A hero of the American Revolution, Lafayette hoped to guide and ultimately control the French Revolution. However, following the Champs de Mars Massacre he was disgraced and never regained the people's confidence. (The New York Public Library Picture Collection)

Lafayette so impressed the Americans that they made him a major general in their army, serving without pay. Army general George Washington became his patron, and a father-

In November 1790 Burke published a book entitled *Reflections of the Revolution in France.* "When ancient opinions and rules of life are taken away," he wrote, "the loss cannot possibly be estimated. From that moment we have no compass to govern us." Such words from

son relationship developed between the two that ended years later, with Washington's death. Lafayette served bravely in numerous campaigns and persuaded King Louis to send financial aid to the colonists. He played an important part in America's victory at the battle of Yorktown, which led to the war's end.

The 24-year-old Lafayette returned to France in 1782. He quickly became a leading light in the liberal movement and helped establish the Estates-General. He was an early advocate of the National Assembly and helped form a plan for a constitutional monarchy. Lafayette hoped a new form of government would give the French people many of the freedoms enjoyed by the new United States of America.

Lafayette's subsequent downfall owed as much to his overriding ambition as to the radicalization of the Revolution. After years in an Austrian prison, in 1799 he returned to a very different France. Napoléon had just assumed power as the first consul. Lafayette refused to help the new leader and worked toward Napoléon's final abdication following the battle of Waterloo in 1815. When the monarchists became a threat again, Lafayette opposed them, championing democracy at home and abroad from Europe to Latin America.

In 1830 he again found himself in a position of power as head of the National Guard. He led a successful revolt against the Bourbon king, Louis XVIII, but when offered the presidency of his country, Lafayette turned it down. In his long life he had learned the many ways that power can corrupt. Unfortunately, the man Lafayette helped make constitutional monarch, Louis-Philippe, ended up betraying his democratic ideals. Lafayette did not live to see France an independent republic. He died in 1834, having devoted much of his life to the cause of freedom.

England's leading liberal were enough to warm the heart of King George III himself. Burke's book was an instant best seller in England and greatly affected both public opinion and government policy toward the French Revolution.

Another born Englishman, as gifted with a pen as Burke, rushed to the Revolution's defense. Thomas Paine had helped the cause of American independence with his memorable pamphlet *Common Sense* a few years earlier. He now attempted to do the same for the French Revolution with his new book *The Rights of Man*, written in direct response to Burke's book. The Girondists were so grateful to Paine that they made him an honorary French citizen in 1792, along with such other champions of liberty as Washington and Polish freedom fighter General Thaddeus Kosciusko.

Although Paine spoke no French, he moved to Paris to observe and participate in the extraordinary events going on there. His presence, however, soon proved am embarrassment to the Mountain. During Louis XVI's trial, Paine suggested that instead of cutting off the king's head, the Convention should ship him off to democratic America, where the fallen monarch might be rehabilitated politically. It wasn't long before Citizen Paine was sitting in a cell in the Luxembourg prison as a foreign "national." "It is ironic," writes historian Arnold Whitridge, "that the man considered a traitor in England was jailed in France for being an Englishman." Paine's release a year later was due largely to the intervention not of the English, but of the new American foreign minister, James Monroe.

By then American support for the French Revolution was waning. Lafayette's flight, France's aggression against its smaller neighbors such as Belgium, and the execution of the king all contributed to American disillusionment. The French Revolution was turning out to be quite a different animal from the American Revolution. Thomas Jefferson, the ultimate apologist for the French Revolution, could marvel early on at "so little innocent blood" shed, but by 1794, rivers of blood were flowing across France. Despite the horrors to come, Jefferson never wavered in his support. Not so Washington. When his Polish friend Kosciusko visited him in 1797, the recently retired president lamented, "The acts of the French . . . ought to warn all nations of their intentions; ought to teach that it is not freedom nor the happiness of men, but an untrammelled ambition and a desire to spread their conquests and to rule everywhere which is the only goal of their measures!"

This fear of Revolutionary ideas spreading abroad, like a pestilence, motivated other European powers to invade France and attempt to crush its revolutionary government. Although Britain had remained neutral in 1792 when France went to war against its neighbors, it changed its position following Louis's death. Anticipating this, the National Convention declared war on Britain and the Dutch Republic on February 1, 1793. In the months to follow, a coalition of nations formed against France. Eventually the coalition included Spain, Russia, Prussia, Austria, parts of Italy, and Portugal. Each nation made a solemn pledge to stay at war with France and support a naval blockade until all territory lost to the French was restored. The ultimate goal of the revolutionaries was no longer in doubt. " . . . It is perfect blindness not to see that in the establishment of the French Republic is included the overthrow of all the other governments of Europe," declared British Foreign Secretary Lord Grenville.

The United States was not a part of this coalition, but its allegiance to the new France was fading fast. The final blow was the arrival in the United States of French envoy and Girondist Edmond Genet. A blundering diplomat, Genet did everything he could to destroy American neutrality. He attempted to issue official commissions to sympathetic Americans and even outfitted privateer ships to enter the war.

Finally, an angry President Washington demanded his recall, and a new envoy was sent to the United States. But Genet did not return to France. He married the daughter of New York governor De Witt Clinton and settled down on a farm on Long Island. The French revolutionary was transformed into a prosperous American capitalist. It was the wisest decision Genet ever made, for in France, the center of power was shifting once more.

CHAPTER 6 NOTES

p. 50   " . . . the liberty of the whole earth . . ." Richard Cobb and Colin Jones, *Voices of the French Revolution*, p. 95.

p. 50   "Are these 'The Rights of Man'? . . ." Cobb and Jones, *Voices of the French Revolution*, p. 158.

p. 52   " . . . The attention of all . . ." Cobb and Jones, *Voices of the French Revolution*, p. 42.

p. 52   "a tribute which I owe . . ." Cobb and Jones, *Voices of the French Revolution*, p. 94.

p. 52   "The revolution . . . in France . . ." Cobb and Jones, *Voices of the French Revolution*, p. 94.

p. 52   "I will not turn them out . . ." Arnold Whitridge, "A Representative of America," *American Heritage*, June 1976. p. 90.

p. 54   "When ancient opinions and rules . . ." Cobb and Jones, *Voices of the French Revolution*, p. 103.

p. 56   "It is ironic . . ." Whitridge, "A Representative of America," p. 91.

p. 56   "The acts of the French . . ." Julian Ursyn Niemcewicz, "A Visit to Mount Vernon," *American Heritage*, February 1965, pp. 68–69.

p. 57   ". . . It is perfect blindness . . ." Cobb and Jones, *Voices of the French Revolution*, p. 177.

THE MOUNTAIN
IS MASTER

"In order to ensure public tranquility, two hundred thousand heads must be cut off."
—Jean-Paul Marat

"I killed one man, in order to save a hundred thousand."
—Charlotte Corday at her trial

Opposition against the Revolution was growing stronger inside France as well as abroad. When insurrection finally exploded in early 1793, it was not the nobles or the clergy who rose up in the greatest numbers, but the poor peasants of the provinces. This counterrevolution started in earnest in the Vendée district on the Bay of Biscay in western France, one of the poorest regions of the country.

The Revolution, for all its rhetoric, had done little to improve the lives of the people there. To the contrary, they had lost more under republican rule than they had under the monarchy. When a new draft law went out in February to raise troops for the European war, it was the last straw. As the rebels of one village put it in a decree: "They [the republicans] have killed our king; chased away our priests; sold the goods of our church; eaten everything we have and now they want to take our bodies . . . no, they shall not have them." If the Vendéans were going to give their blood for France, it would be for a cause they believed in—the overthrow of the Revolutionary government.

On March 11, an army of peasants, numbering in the thousands, marched into the market town of Machecoul. Armed only with farm implements, they killed 40 local republicans and imprisoned 400 people. Many of these prisoners were constitutional priests, landowners and their servants, all of whom were later executed as ruthlessly as the prisoners in the September Massacres. The revolutionaries were getting a taste of their own brutality.

Other uprisings occurred in towns throughout the Vendée. The insurrectionists, led by poor aristocrats as desperate as the peasants, quickly formed a guerilla army using the weapons left behind by the fleeing republicans. Their strategy was a sound one—strike with lightning speed and then fade quickly into the countryside. The success of the Vendéans incited insurrections in many other regions, most notably Britanny.

The war outside France was also heating up. The victory of Valmy had made the French overconfident. The war to save France had now become the war to liberate subjects from their masters in every European country. France soon found itself pitted against all of Europe—a war it could not possibly win.

But the motives of the National Convention were not all idealistic. The war was also seen as an opportunity to replenish the dwindling revolutionary coffers. Invading French armies quickly confiscated property belonging to the church and foreign governments. Visiting war commissioners plundered captive Belgium. General Dumouriez protested this blatant extortion, fearing it would only inflame the Belgian people, who might have expected better from the land of liberty.

The government, under pressure from the Mountain, ordered Dumouriez to invade Holland, which he reluctantly did. Undermanned and unable to defend the Belgian border, Dumouriez's troops were defeated by the advancing Austrians just east of Brussels. Dumouriez, whose Girondist party was losing power, was thoroughly disillusioned. Like Lafayette before him, this general decided his real enemy now was the Revolutionary government. He tried to negotiate with the Austrians, hoping to join forces with them and take Paris. His soldiers, however, refused, and a mutiny broke out. Without an army, Dumouriez took the only course left open to him. He fled to Austria.

The Mountain did not view the schemes and desertion of the army's supreme commander as the act of one man, but rather as proof of a vast conspiracy to overthrow the government. The Girondists were implicated in this conspiracy and besieged from all sides. Armed with Robespierre's organizational skills, Danton's eloquence and Marat's bitter invective, the Mountain launched a frontal assault on its political foes. Marches, demonstrations and public manifestoes were masterfully orchestrated to bring the Girondists to their knees. The Mountain used the Commune and the sans-culottes to these ends, but was careful to keep them under control. They did not want another massacre in the streets to loosen anarchy in Paris. If there was to be violence, it would be state sanctioned and legitimized. Danton put it succinctly when he said, "Let us embody terror so as to prevent the people from doing so."

To this end the Revolutionary Tribunal was established to try all crimes against the state. Tribunal members would not be elected by the people, but appointed by the National Convention, and their power would be absolute. Watch committees were set up in every neighborhood to ferret out and expel any foreigners suspected of counterrevolutionary activities. On April 6 the General Defense Committee set up by the Girondists was replaced by a Committee of Public Safety. The charge of this nine-member body, led by Danton, was more ambiguous than the Tribunal's. Its purpose was to "protect the public safety" from enemies both in and outside France. The Committee soon employed a shadowy network of informers and spies to achieve these ends. No one was safe from suspicion. A careless word of criticism spoken against the government could put one in prison or worse.

The Girondists had no representation on the Committee of Public Safety. Bit by bit, the Jacobins were shutting them out of power. The Girondists, however, were not going to give up without a fight. They decided to strike out at the Mountain's most conspicuous target, Marat. This "croaking toad," as one Girondist described him, had accused the

Girondists of being France's "greatest enemies" and the power behind the counterrevolution. Marat had been made president of the Jacobin Club, a position of power he was expected to use to its full potential to strike out at his enemies. By destroying Marat, the Girondists hoped to weaken the Mountain and regain some of their power.

But they had waited too long to strike. Marat was riding a crest of popularity in Paris. He was cheered heartily as he entered the courtroom to face the charges against him. His trial was brief. The Revolutionary Tribunal acquitted Marat, and his supporters carried him out of the courtroom on their shoulders.

The Girondists had played their last card. François Hanriot, a sans-culotte leader and a notorious drunkard, was appointed the new head of the National Guard. On May 31 the Convention ordered him to shut the gates of the city and arrest most of the leading Girondists. Jean-Marie Roland escaped and went into hiding. Other Girondists fled to the provinces and joined the counterrevolution they had so often been accused of starting.

The Mountain was now the master of France. At first, its members used their power with great care. Even the fanatical Saint-Just called for moderation. "Proscribe [punish] those who have fled to take up arms . . ." he told the Convention. "Judge the rest and pardon the majority." To show that their hearts were with the people, the Jacobins sold land confiscated from émigrés to peasants through generous loans. By doing this, they created a whole new class of small landowners who would thrive in France for 150 years. The Jacobins also created a more liberal constitution to replace the old, discarded one. It was daringly democratic for its time, but it was set aside until conditions in the nation were stabilized.

Danton and Robespierre were the people's heroes, but neither enjoyed Marat's popularity among the sans-culottes. His acquittal had raised him to new heights of fame. However, Marat was hated as intensely as he was loved. Many Girondists had fled from Paris to Caen, a city known for its counterrevolutionary sympathies. Among the most fervent Girondist sympathizers in Caen was Charlotte Corday, the daughter of a poor nobleman. Like a latter-day Joan of Arc, Corday saw herself as appointed by God to deliver France from the scourge of the Jacobins. And one man, above all, embodied all that she hated.

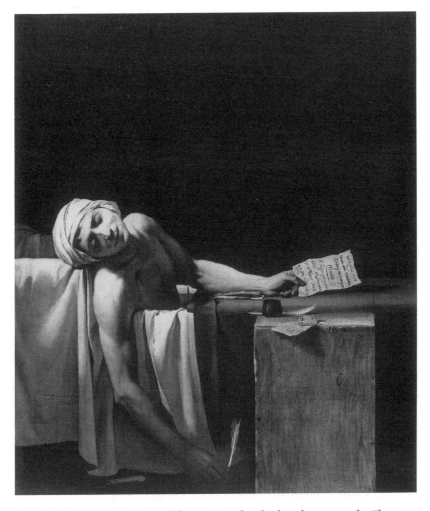

David's Death of Marat *is one of the great works of political propaganda. The artist used Marat's embalmed corpse as his model. The body was later exhibited to the public for three days before the ceremonious funeral.* (The Bettmann Archive)

On July 11, 1793 Corday arrived in Paris. Two days later, she left her rented room and bought a kitchen knife with a five-inch steel blade at a cutler's shop. She slipped it discreetly under her skirt and proceeded to Marat's home near the Cordeliers Club.

On her arrival at Marat's house, Corday was met by the sister of his common-law wife, Simone Evrard. Corday asked to see Marat and was curtly turned away. She returned to her room and wrote a note she

Jean-Paul Marat
(1743–1793)

The real Marat was far removed from this idealized portrait. He dressed in rags and flaunted his uncouth behavior in public. Marat frightened and distressed the middle-class delegates of the Convention, but he was embraced by the common people who saw him as their hero. (The New York Public Library Picture Collection)

If the Royal Academy of Science had accepted Jean-Paul Marat as a member, the French Revolution might have lost one of its most radical leaders. Like Adolf Hitler, who turned to politics only after failing as an artist, Marat became a political activist when his dream of becoming a great scientist was shattered.

Born in Boudry, Switzerland, this spokesman of the common man began his career as a physician to the cream of Parisian society. Marat was a practitioner of electrotherapy, a fashionable but questionable treatment that used electricity to cure every malady of the day. He also wrote books on a variety

hoped would arouse Marat's interest. It said she had important information for him concerning the Girondists in Caen. She delivered the note and waited for a reply. None came. Undaunted, she returned to Marat's house about 7 P.M. The place was a flurry of activity as Marat's radical paper, *L'Ami du peuple* (Friend of the People), was about to go to press. Corday found the doors unguarded and entered the house. Once inside, Evrard spotted her. Corday stated her business in a loud voice, hoping that Marat would hear. He did and ordered Evrard to let her in.

of subjects, from physiology to politics. When Marat applied for membership to the French Academy of Science, however, he was rejected, and his theories on healing were ridiculed.

An embittered Marat vowed revenge. He quickly saw the approaching revolution as a means to that end. He founded a newspaper, *L'Ami du peuple* (Friend of the People), and in its pages he attacked the great and powerful. As the Revolution progressed, Marat focused his hatred on the National Assembly for not being radical enough in its reforms. He called for a government that was totally democratic. Yet for Marat it didn't matter who was in power and what they did. All authority was fair game for him, until he himself was master of France.

Marat's power grew with that of the sans-culottes of Paris, who saw this unkempt, ugly little man with his diseased, yellowed skin as their champion. In September 1792 Marat was elected to the National Convention, where he called for the king's death and the deposing of the Girondists. Feared and hated as a madman by many moderates, Marat was as crazy as a fox. During his trial before the Revolutionary Tribunal, he once pulled out a pistol and threatened to shoot himself if he was convicted. He wasn't convicted, of course, and became a bigger hero than ever.

After Charlotte Corday ended his meteoric rise with a kitchen knife a few months later, Marat's body was interred in the Panthéon, and his heart was suspended from the ceiling of the Cordelier Club for public veneration. In the end, he didn't need the French Academy after all.

Corday was startled by the sight of the man she had come to kill. Marat sat in a tub of kaolin solution to soothe his wrinkled, peeling skin. A plank laid across the tub served as his writing desk. He gestured for Corday to sit on a nearby stool. For 15 minutes they talked. Corday gave Marat the names of the Girondist plotters in Caen, which he carefully recorded. When she finished, he smiled and said, "Good, in a few days I will have them all guillotined." With that, Corday pulled the knife from her clothing and stabbed him in the side.

Charlotte Corday
(1768–1793)

Charlotte Corday was a most unlikely assassin, who gained great sympathy abroad for her act. She showed no fear or misgivings during her brief trial. In a last letter to her father she wrote, "I beg you to forget me or rather to rejoice at my fate. The cause is good." (The New York Public Library Picture Collection)

"Her beautiful face was so calm, that one would have said she was a statue," wrote an adoring observer as he watched Marat's assassin take her last trip to the guillotine. "For eight days I was in love with Charlotte Corday."

This handsome young woman from Caen evoked both great sympathy and great hatred for her assassination of one of the Revolution's greatest leaders. It is not surprising to learn that Corday was related to the great French dramatist Pierre Corneille, for she

"Help, help, dear friends!" cried the stricken man. One of Marat's assistants threw a chair at the fleeing Corday, and another hurled himself on her. Evrard rushed to Marat, but it was too late. The man who had incited thousands to spill blood now lay dying in his own.

Marat in death was even a more powerful force than in life. His embalmed body lay in state for three days while hundreds of mourners passed before it. The funeral that followed was a national event; so was the brief but dramatic trial of Charlotte Corday. The beautiful young woman from Caen was the object of public revulsion and fascination. When asked by a prosecutor what she hoped to achieve by Marat's

was as masterful at theatrics as the man she murdered.

Corday's family was old nobility that had fallen on hard times. She believed fervently in the republic but saw the extremism of the Mountain as destroying it. When some Girondists fled to Caen, their presence inspired Corday to destroy Marat, the man she saw as most responsible for their downfall. She planned to kill him before the nation's eyes on the Convention floor, but was forced to change her strategy when Marat stayed home, nursing his painful skin disease.

During her trial, the prosecution tried in vain to get her to admit she was merely a tool of a Girondist conspiracy. "I alone conceived the plan and executed it," she said proudly. "Do you think you have killed all the Marats?" the prosecutor asked her. "With this one dead, the others, perhaps, will be afraid," she replied.

In fact, her act contributed to the establishment of the Reign of Terror. Despite the failure of her cause, this strange, idealistic woman left behind her a legacy of commitment and courage. As she mounted the steps to the guillotine, the executioner felt sorry for her and tried to shield her from seeing the blade. Corday would have none of that. "I've never seen one before," she told him. "In the circumstances, I'm rather curious."

death, she calmly replied, "Peace. Now that he is dead, peace will return to my country."

She went to the guillotine the following day, blissfully ignorant of the fact that she had not killed a tyrant but created a martyr. Marat in life had been a loose cannon, a dangerous man whom the Jacobins feared more than the Girondists. He had lived only to further his own fame and the power that had been given him by the people. Now that power would be used to further the ends of the Jacobins.

Thus, one of the most famous assassinations in modern times became brilliant political propaganda. Charlotte Corday may have insisted at her trial that she acted alone, but the Revolutionary Tribunal proclaimed the murder was final proof of a vicious, nationwide conspiracy. The brief notice posted on Marat's door said it all: "Weep but remember that he must be avenged."

Marat was not the only hero of the Revolution whose career was cut short in that hot July of 1793. Danton had been secretly working for a peace settlement with France's enemies to end the war. When this was discovered, the "Lord High Sans-Culotte" was discredited and lost reelection to the Committee of Public Safety. He and several moderate committee members were replaced by Saint-Just and Georges Couthon, a disabled lawyer and another firm follower of Robespierre.

Then, on July 27, another member conveniently resigned for health reasons and Robespierre himself took a seat on the Committee of Public Safety. With Marat dead and Danton disgraced, this 35-year-old lawyer with a puritanical streak now reigned supreme. The time had come to cement his power in blood.

CHAPTER 7 NOTES

p. 59   "In order to ensure public tranquility . . ." Susan Banfield, *The Rights of Man, The Reign of Terror: The Story of the French Revolution*, p. 119.

p. 59   "I killed one man . . ." David Dowd, *The French Revolution*, p. 118.

pp. 59–60 "They have killed our king . . ." Simon Schama, *Citizens: A Chronicle of the French Revolution*, p. 694.

p. 62   "Proscribe those who have fled . . ." N.S. Pratt, *The French Revolution*, p. 87.

p. 66   "Her beautiful face . . ." Schama, *Citizens*, p. 741.

p. 67   "I alone conceived the plan . . ." Schama, *Citizens* p. 739.

p. 67   "I've never seen one . . ." Dowd, *The French Revolution*, p. 118.

p. 67   "Peace. Now that he is dead . . ." Richard Cobb and Colin Jones, *Voices of the French Revolution*, p. 192.

p. 68   "Weep but remember . . ." Schama, *Citizens*, p. 741.

LET TERROR REIGN

"Still more heads and every day more heads fall! . . . What majesty! What imposing tone! How completely edifying . . . What cement for the Republic."
> —barber surgeon Achard in letter from Lyon to his brother in Paris

"My turn now!"
> —Danton before the guillotine

S_{ay} "French Revolution" and the image that pops into most people's heads is a cart full of condemned prisoners approaching a bloodied guillotine, as a crowd of dirty-faced sans-culottes cheer and jeer them. In reality, the infamous Reign of Terror, initiated by Robespierre and his cohorts, lasted a little less than a year—from September 1793 to July 1794. During this brief time, over 2,500 people went to their deaths before "the blade of the law" in Paris alone. Tens of thousands of others were executed in other cities and towns throughout France.

When considering this most infamous period of the Revolution, the most important question is not how it happened but why it happened at all. The answer brings us to the very heart of what the French Revolution stood for. Death and violence, as a number of historians have pointed out, was not a by-product of the Revolution, but the very essence of it. Organized killing was seen as necessary to wipe out the Revolution's enemies and make the republic secure. The shedding of blood, in Revolutionary art and literature, took on an almost religious aura, a sacrificial purging of the state to allow it to grow and flourish.

By the summer of 1793, the enemies of the Revolution seemed to be everywhere. Foreign armies were pounding at the gates of France, insurrectionists now controlled much of the countryside and fanatics such as Charlotte Corday could casually walk in off the street and kill a Marat in his own bath. To secure power, keep order and save the state from anarchy, the Committee of Public Safety, in conjunction with the Revolutionary Tribunal, adopted a policy of terror. "Let terror be the order of the day," declared Danton, who would later come to reconsider his words. Through terror, fear and intimidation, the Jacobin government hoped to bring order to a lawless land and establish a strong and virtuous society. Once order was firmly established, the Reign of Terror would end. At least that is the way it was planned.

The machinery of the Terror was swift and terrible. One night a person might be safe asleep in bed. Suddenly there would be a knock at the door and an armed guard would awake the person and read a battery of charges against him or her. The accuser might be a neighbor, a friend or even a close relative. The crimes could range from working as an active counterrevolutionary to something as trivial as wearing the white cockade of the Bourbons. For the latter offense a person could be shot within 24 hours.

After being told the crime, the accused would be given a few moments to dress and say good-bye to loved ones. From home, the prisoner was taken to a place of detention. There were over 50 of these makeshift prisons in Paris, including former schools, soldiers' barracks, religious convents and even a library. Conditions were often crude. Many prisoners were confined to tiny cells and slept on straw-covered floors, but in some prisons aristocrats could dine elegantly in more pleasant surroundings before going to their deaths.

The accused could languish in prison for weeks or months before being brought to trial. The worst part was not knowing when the day of judgment would come. Every time the prison door opened, hearts beat fast and bodies broke into cold sweats. To take their mind off what lay ahead, prisoners passed the time in reading, conversation, letter writing and even music making. (One prison boasted a string quartet.) Male and female prisoners could mix freely, and some had affairs. Romance was quickened by the fact that a pregnant woman could not be executed until after she had delivered her child.

When the prisoner's time of trial came, he or she was taken from the prison with up to 50 other prisoners and brought before the Revolutionary Tribunal. There the accused was given the opportunity to offer a defense before the judges. The verdict was not always predetermined. Of the 5,000 people tried by the Tribunal in Paris between 1793 and 1795, 2,750 were sentenced to death, while 2,250 were acquitted. In

The worst part of prison life during the Reign of Terror was waiting for the end. Here the jailkeeper calls out the names of those who have been condemned to death. A group of aristocrats react to the dreaded news with shock, grief and stoic resignation. (The Bettmann Archive)

either case, there was no appeal to a higher court. The Tribunal's power was absolute.

If the prisoner was found guilty and sentenced to death, justice was swift. The condemned was brought to a holding cell where guards shaved the hair off the neck and tore open the prisoner's shirt to make the work of the guillotine easier. By late afternoon, often on the same day, the dreaded tumbrels, small, two-wheeled, horse-drawn carts, arrived to take the condemned on their last journey. Ten to 15 prisoners were herded standing into one tumbrel and taken to the Place de la Revolution where the guillotine awaited them.

One by one the condemned, hands bound behind them, mounted the steep stairs to the guillotine, sometimes accompanied by a priest, who would offer up prayers for their souls. Those poor wretches who trembled or cried on their last walk were jeered and hooted, while those who kept up a brave front to the end could elicit admiration and even sympathy from the crowd. Whatever the disposition of the condemned, the mob who came to watch enjoyed the spectacle enormously and would sit in stands like fans at a sporting event. The men cheered and laughed; many of the women passed the time before the main event knitting, like the heartless Madame Defarge in Charles Dickens's novel *A Tale of Two Cities*. These women, called *tricoteuses*, French for "knitters," were dubbed by royalists the "furies of the guillotine."

Once on the scaffold, the executioner helped the condemned stretch out on the wooden plank. The head was thrust in the "little window" and the blade fell. Blood gushed from the headless torso down to the covering of hay below the guillotine. The head dropped into a waiting basket and was then held up for public view by the executioner, an integral part of the ritual. The body was rolled off the plank and the blade raised back up by a winch and readied for the next victim.

The roll call of the condemned included people from every level of society. While aristocrats were originally the main targets of the Terror, soon the vast majority of prisoners were ordinary citizens, some of them even sans-culottes. Two of the most famous victims were women— Marie-Antoinette and the darling of the Girondists, Madame Roland. Both women faced death bravely and unrepentant. "The bitch was audacious and insolent right to the very end," wrote the radical journalist Jacques René Hébert about the execution of the queen. "However, her legs failed her at the moment of being tipped over to shake the hot hand." Hébert, who replaced Marat as the firebrand of the people, specialized in sick humor and obscenities in his inflammatory newspaper *Le Père Duchesne* (Father Duchesne).[1] Hébert's politics were so far to the left that he regularly attacked the Committee of Public Safety for being too soft.

Even those who escaped arrest and trial were often doomed. When Jean-Marie Roland, still in hiding, received the news that his wife had been executed, he tied his sword to a tree and ran into it. The suicide note found by his body read, "I no longer desire to remain in a world covered with crime."

As the Girondists were going to their doom, time was running out for the counterrevolutionaries. The Vendéans were successful in keeping the republicans at bay as long as they confined their fighting to their own region. But when they extended their civil war to other parts of the country, they found themselves outnumbered and overwhelmed by republican troops. The Vendéans fought their last major battle in October 1793 and by December were utterly defeated. The revolutionary army was merciless in its reprisals. "There is no more Vendée, citizens," General François-Joseph Westermann could proudly report to the Committee of Public Safety, "it has perished under our free sword along with its women and children. I have just buried it in the marshes and mud of Savenay . . . I have no prisoners with which to reproach myself."

Westermann was not exaggerating. Up to a third of the region's people perished in mass executions whose savagery would not be equaled until our own century. Thousands of insurrectionists were tied in pairs, loaded into boats and drowned in the river Loire, an act humorously referred to as "republican baptisms." Mapmakers changed the name of the area to "Vengé," French for "Avenged."

---

1. Father Duchesne was a popular fictional character of the time who hung around fairgrounds, smoking a pipe and doling out commonsense advice to anyone who would listen. Under Hébert's guidance, *Le Père Duchesne* became the most popular radical newspaper in France and a sans-culotte favorite.

Contrary to popular belief, only a small fraction of the Terror's victims died by the guillotine. The vast majority were shot, stabbed, drowned in boats or hurled from tall buildings, as these unfortunate Vendéans. If the fall didn't kill them, they were sure to drown in the waters below. (The Bettmann Archive)

Other centers of rebellion, including Marseilles and Toulon, were treated just as harshly. The city of Lyon was nearly obliterated. Sixteen hundred homes were reduced to rubble. A column erected on the spot read simply:

Lyon made war on liberty

Lyon is no more

In one hideous example of expediency, 60 prisoners at Lyon were tied together with ropes and shot at with a cannon. The guillotine lopped off heads at a feverish pitch. On one day, 12 heads were chopped off in five minutes!

The fall of the insurrectionists coincided with France's triumph over its foreign enemies. The military command now lay in the capable hands of Lazore Carnot, a military engineer and member of the Committee of Public Safety. Carnot strengthened the army in numbers and morale. He replaced aristocrat officers with common men who came up through the ranks. He skillfully marshaled his troops into massive units where sheer numbers made up for inexperience. By the end of 1793, France had regained nearly all its lost territory and driven its enemies outside its borders.

Peace was restored, and the threat of foreign invasion and internal strife was removed. The Terror, however, showed no signs of subsiding. On October 10, 1793 Saint-Just made perhaps his greatest speech in the Convention, urging no mercy for traitors. "Between the people and their enemies there can be nothing in common but the sword," he declared. "We must govern by iron those who cannot be governed by justice . . . It is impossible for revolutionary laws to be executed unless the government itself is truly revolutionary."

Among the lingering enemies of France the radicals now singled out religion. For centuries the church's hierarchy had aligned itself with the power of the state. It was seen early on in the Revolution as a reactionary force to be attacked. Now radicals such as Hébert attacked the very core of Christianity. They sought to obliterate every trace of religion as completely as they had the strongholds of the insurrectionists. Churches were shut down. The pope and other church leaders were hanged in effigy. Shrines were desecrated and priests forced to marry. Atheism became the new state religion, and the Cathedral of Notre Dame, the greatest place of worship in all France, was transformed into a "Temple of Reason," where the church saints were replaced by busts of "Saints" Voltaire and Rousseau.

The height of this process of de-Christianization was reached when a new revolutionary calendar was announced. The traditional

Marie-Antoinette
(1755–1793)

The gaunt, gray-haired woman who mounted the steps to the guillotine on October 16, 1793 was almost unrecognizable as the handsome, vivacious queen who had ruled France only a few years earlier. But what she had lost in looks, Marie-Antoinette made up for in dignity. When she accidentally stepped on the executioner's foot on the scaffold, she graciously apologized.

No woman was more hated by the people in Revolutionary France than Queen Marie-Antoinette. Among other sobriquets, her enemies called her the "Austrian Woman," "Madame Deficit," "Madame Veto" and after her husband's death, the "Widow Capet." (The New York Public Library Picture Collection)

France's last queen had been a feckless monarch in the classic mode. The daughter of Francis I, leader of the Holy Roman Empire, she had been groomed to rule from infancy. Marie was married to France's crown prince at 15, and four years later became queen. She quickly earned a reputation for extrava-

seven-day week was replaced with a ten-day week. Sunday, the traditional Christian day of worship, disappeared, along with all holy days and feast days. The tenth day of the week was called a décade and was designated as a day of rest, but not worship. The new calendar retained the twelve months, but each now had 30 days. The five remaining days of the year were humorously called "sans-culottides." Danton's friend, the poet Fabre d'Eglantine, replaced

gance and pleasure-seeking. She had her own fantasy village built at Versailles where she and her court could play at being blushing milkmaids and rustic swains. Her foreignness only added to her unpopularity with her subjects, who referred to her as the "Austrian Woman."

Motherhood made the queen more domestic and drew her closer to her husband Louis, whom she had previously found dull and boorish. A serious Marie-Antoinette, however, proved more dangerous than a frivolous one. The queen took to meddling in affairs of state, scheming to get reforming ministers such as Necker fired, and telling Louis to stand firm when revolution broke out in 1789.

Because she was a convenient target, Marie-Antoinette was blamed for everything wrong in pre-Revolutionary France, even the errors made solely by her husband. Many of the stories spread about her in her lifetime are untrue. She never said "Let them eat cake" when the people were rioting over the price of bread. Rousseau attributed the remark to a certain "princess" two years before the future queen set foot in France.

In 1794, with her husband dead and her children taken from her, Marie-Antoinette languished in prison, an object of scorn and humiliation. At her trial, she was accused of seducing her own son, a cruel and unfounded charge. She was guilty of charges of treason, however, having given military secrets to Austria in a desperate attempt to end the Revolution with a foreign invasion.

Spoiled and willful, Marie-Antoinette refused to believe the Revolution was anything more than a few villains leading the people of France astray. It was an illusion she carried with her to her grave.

the Roman names of the months with "politically correct" names that reflected the republic's love of the natural world. Thus Nivose (December 21–January 19) was the "snowy month," Germinal (March 21–April 19) the "budding month," Thermidor (July 19–August 17) the "month of heat," and Vendémiarie (September 22–October 21) the "vintage month," when grapes were harvested for wine.

Robespierre, while he supported the new calendar, was troubled by the antireligious campaign. Although not a Christian, Robespierre firmly believed in a Supreme Being who guided the Revolution. Atheism, he believed, could lead only to immorality and the breakdown of the state. Besides this, other Christian countries were viewing de-Christianization with horror, making France a potential pariah in the European community. Robespierre accused the anti-Christian extremists of being one more manifestation of a foreign conspiracy to overthrow the government. At Robespierre's urging in December 1793, the Convention passed a decree of freedom of worship, reestablishing religion and condemning the extremists.

This decree further dramatized the growing division between the Jacobins and the radical leaders of the Commune that had helped them come to power. Now that the Jacobins were running the government they were viewed with suspicion and criticized just as the Girondists had been before them. Led by the firebrand Hébert, the Commune blamed the Committee of Public Safety for continuing food shortages and spiraling inflation.

Meanwhile, on the right, the Committee found itself under attack from one of its former allies. Danton had retired to his country home with his new wife after his dismissal from the Committee of Public Safety. He returned to the capital in November 1793 a changed man. The popular leader who had a year earlier joined forces with Robespierre and declared "I now abandon moderation because prudence has its limits" was beginning to see that the Terror had its limits too. Danton believed that with the war won and the insurrectionists crushed, the Terror had outlived its usefulness. The time had come, he felt, to stop chopping off heads and start rebuilding the country. A political pragmatist at heart, Danton could see the people were wearying of executions and lofty Jacobin rhetoric. They wanted full stomachs and money in their pockets. Danton's friends, such as the courageous journalist Camille Desmoulins, openly criticized the methods of the Terror and called for its end.

The Committee realized that until the Hébertists on the left and the Dantonists on the right were silenced, its power would not be secure. Hébert made himself an easy victim. Filled with overconfidence (his newspaper was now the most widely read in all France), he called for an insurrection on March 4, 1794. In response, Saint-Just delivered another blood-stirring speech to the Convention, pressuring members to pass a law condemning any persons who criticized the government. Hébert and his followers were quickly rounded up, tried and condemned. The man who had turned the guillotine into a national joke was not laughing now. He went to his death weeping and cringing, hooted and jeered by the same sans-culottes whose cause he had triumphed. His death left the Commune stunned and leaderless.

Hébert was gone, but Danton was another matter. The lion of the Revolution was no longer in the seat of power, but he remained a powerful personage. Besides this, he and Robespierre had been close friends. Robespierre did his best to persuade his old comrade to renounce his moderate followers and support the Committee of Public Safety. Danton, defiantly independent, refused and his fate was sealed. The members of the committee signed the order for his arrest. Robespierre reluctantly was the last to sign.

On the evening of March 31, Danton was arrested at his home and charged with anti-Jacobinism, royalism and corruption.[2] Arriving at the Luxembourg prison, Danton greeted his friends already behind bars with customary good humor: "Gentlemen, I had hoped to get you out of here. I'm afraid instead that I am to be shut up with you."

The trial that followed was a mockery of justice, but for once the Revolutionary Tribunal had met its match. Danton spoke out against those who would destroy him with fierce eloquence. "People," he declared to the hushed courtroom, "you will judge me when you have heard me; my voice will not only be heard by you but throughout all of France."

When the court tried to stop his passionate outbursts by ringing a bell, Danton replied, "The voice of a man who has to defend both his life and honor must vanquish the sound of your little bell." But the Tribunal would not be denied its pound of flesh, however eloquent its victim's defense. Under a court order, Danton and his fellow defendants were removed from the hall and quickly condemned in their absence.

---

2. Danton was guilty only of the last of these charges. In his years as a public official, he was not above taking bribes to support his lavish lifestyle.

Antoine Laurent de Lavoisier
(1743–1794)

Lavoisier's death during the Terror was a tragic loss to the world of science and only highlighted the senselessness of the killing. Note the inset showing the chemist conducting one of his experiments with oxygen, while the guillotine lurks ominously in the background. (The New York Public Library Picture Collection)

Queens, aristocrats and commoners were not the only ones condemned during the Reign of Terror. Writers, artists and scientists lost their heads too. Among the most celebrated of these was Antoine Laurent de Lavoisier, perhaps the greatest French scientist of the 18th century.

Lavoisier was born in Paris to a family of nobility and studied the physical sciences at College Mazarin. At 23 he was awarded a gold medal by the French Academy of Sciences for a sensible plan of lighting the city's streets. It was chemistry, however, where Lavoisier made his major contribution to science. He unlocked the secrets of fire, rec-

The Lord High Sans-Culotte faced death with the same devil-may-care attitude that he had lived by. His final journey to the guillotine on April 6, 1794 was faithfully described by an observer:

Danton was the first to climb into the first of the three carts which were to take the group to the Place de la Revolution. The loading

ognizing oxygen as the key ingredient. He also proved that matter can be neither created nor destroyed, only changed from one form to another—the law of conservation of matter. In 1789, on the eve of the Revolution, Lavoisier wrote the first modern chemistry textbook, *Elements of Chemistry.*

However, he had a second career that did not bode him well in the new republic. Lavoisier was a member of Farmer-General, an age-old financial company that collected government taxes. Because of this he was branded an "enemy of the people" and arrested. This was unfair, for Lavoisier had worked tirelessly to improve the lives of the poor as a member of government, agricultural and financial organizations.

Among the new leaders of France, Lavoisier had an archenemy. When Jean-Paul Marat applied for membership to the Academy of Sciences, Lavoisier was one of the members who questioned his qualifications and blocked his election. It was something Marat never forgot. Twelve years later, in his newspaper, Marat called Lavoisier a "companion of tyrants" who should be hanged from "the next lamp-post." At his trial, friends pleaded for the life of the 51-year-old scientist. "The Republic does not need scientists" was the chief justice's chilly reply.

Lavoisier's death was a tragic loss. If he had lived, he might had added immeasurably to the world's store of scientific knowledge. The French mathematician Joseph-Louis Lagrange put it best when he wrote, "It took but a moment to cut off his head but it will take a century to produce another like it."

took over an hour because Camille Desmoulins struggled a long time with the executioner, and knocked him down twice. . . . During this time Danton was laughing in the cart and nodding to the other condemned men, who were by now bound and placed in their carts, to show that he was being kept waiting too long. . . . Seeing the procession pass, a woman in the Rue St-Honoré looked at Danton and exclaimed, "How ugly he is!" He smiled at her and said, "There's no point in telling me that now, I shan't be much longer."

After watching his friends go before him, Danton bounded up the steps. His last witticism was saved for the executioner. "Show my head to the people," he told him. "It is worth seeing."

The Terror's last enemy was gone. Now, like a vicious scorpion, it would turn its deadly stinger on itself.

CHAPTER 8 NOTES

p. 69   "Still more heads . . ." Simon Schama, *Citizens: A Chronicle of the French Revolution*, p. 783.

p. 69   "My turn now!" Richard Cobb and Colin Jones, *Voices of the French Revolution*, p. 218.

p. 72   "The bitch was audacious . . ." Schama, *Citizens*, p. 800.

p. 73   "I no longer desire . . ." Schama, *Citizens*, p. 803.

p. 73   "There is no more Vendée . . ." Schama, *Citizens*, p. 788.

p. 75   "Lyon made war . . ." Schama, *Citizens*, p. 780.

p. 75   "Between the people and their enemies . . ." Schama, *Citizens*, p. 766–67.

p. 78   "I now abandon moderation . . ." Susan Banfield, *The Rights of Man, the Reign of Terror: The Story of the French Revolution*, p.131.

p. 79   "Gentlemen, I had hoped . . ." David Dowd, *The French Revolution*, p. 135.

p. 79   "People, you will judge me . . ." and "The voice of a man . . ." Schama, *Citizens*, p. 818.

p. 80   "Danton was the first . . ." Cobb and Jones, *Voices of the French Revolution*, p. 218.

p. 81   "It took but a moment . . ." Jay E. Greene, *One Hundred Great Scientists*, p. 148.

p. 82   "Show my head . . ." Dowd, *The French Revolution*, p. 136.

DOWNFALL OF A VIRTUOUS TYRANT

"Any individual who usurps the nation's sovereignty shall be immediately put to death by free men."
—Robespierre

"Down with the tyrant!"
—rallying cry of Convention members opposing Robespierre

The downfall of the Hébertists and the Dantonists might have seemed a good reason for the Jacobins to end the Terror, but nothing of the kind happened. A young woman, aspiring to become another Charlotte Corday, showed up at Robespierre's home armed with two knives. She never reached her intended victim, but another assassin did wound committee member Jean-Marie Collot d'Herbois. There was a question as to whether the real target was again Robespierre. These brushes with death convinced Robespierre that

ies of the state were still at large. In fact, France was more stable and
   re than it had been in years. Yet at the very moment when the need for
the Terror was diminishing, it was intensified to a frightening degree.

In June 1794 a decree widened the definition of who was a "public
enemy." Now almost anyone could be accused of being a traitor to France.
Those prisoners coming before the Revolutionary Tribunal were no
longer allowed legal defense and, in most cases, couldn't even call forth
witnesses to help their case. Most ominous of all, once the Tribunal found
a person guilty, it could pronounce only one sentence—death.

What followed has been appropriately called the "Great Terror."
During this 49-day period nearly 1,400 people were executed in Paris,
averaging almost 200 victims a week. More people went to the guillotine in this short time than had in the previous 15 months! Whole
families—men, women and children—went to their doom. By now the
spectacle of death had lost its novelty. To play down the entertainment
aspect of the executions, the guillotine was moved from the Place de
la Revolution to the outskirts of Paris.

The people were not the only ones weary of Robespierre's "republic
of virtue." After months of working day and night to keep the machinery
of terror running smoothly, the Committee of Public Safety was exhausted. With one threat after another removed, the Committee lost
its sense of purpose. By the summer of 1794, it was no longer a united
group of dedicated men, but a collection of individuals in constant
conflict with one another. Petty jealousies and personal differences
began to surface. Carnot, Collot d'Herbois and other Committee
members began to look on Robespierre with a mixture of envy and fear.
Now the president of the Convention, Robespierre was becoming a
power unto himself. Was he planning to turn the Terror against his
colleagues and rule as supreme dictator of France?

Their suspicions seemed confirmed by an extraordinary event that
took place on June 8, 1794. As the crowning touch of his campaign
against de-Christianization, Robespierre announced a grand "Festival
of the Supreme Being." It was an extravagant pageant designed by the
artist David and would assemble the French people to celebrate their
"bonds of universal brotherhood." No pains were spared to make this
a memorable occasion. A procession of Convention deputies marched
into the Tuileries gardens to burn an effigy of atheism. Under the effigy

a statue of wisdom appeared, as if by magic. An artificial mountain, made of plaster and cardboard, was erected on the Champs de Mars. Robespierre, the Supreme Being's high priest, descended from the mountain to meet the people. One Convention deputy, Marc-Antoine Baudot, described the scene:

> He [Robespierre] wore his usual light blue coat and carried a posy of flowers in his hand. People noticed that there was a considerable gap between his colleagues and himself. Some ascribe this to simple deference, others think that Robespierre was using it to underline his sovereignty. I am inclined to think that it was due to detestation of Robespierre.

At least one sans-culotte in the crowd agreed with this assessment. "Look at the bastard," he cried. "It's not enough to be master, he wants to be God as well."

A god does not need to consult with mere mortals, and when differences with Carnot and others on the Committee led to a violent argument, Robespierre simply stayed home and stopped attending meetings. For two weeks he was not seen in public. He thought by staying away he would put fear into the hearts of his enemies and drive them into submission. In reality, he was giving them the opportunity to hatch a conspiracy against him.

The dissension within the Committee of Public Safety emboldened the deputies of the Convention. Fear and hatred of Robespierre gave the anti-Robespierrists on the Committee common cause with the majority in the Convention, and they formed an uneasy alliance. The plot of Thermidor came to a head on July 26 (Thermidor 8) when Robespierre returned to the Convention. The next 72 hours would prove to be among the most critical in five years of revolution.

If the Thermidorians had been conspiring, so had Robespierre. He launched into a speech on the Convention floor denying all desire to make himself dictator and denounced his enemies. He refused to name names, but promised to do so the following day. The conspirators knew the moment had come to act. It was either them or Robespierre.

At 11 A.M. on July 27, Robespierre arrived at the Convention Hall with his two stalwart lieutenants, Saint-Just and Couthon. Saint-Just rose to deliver the coup de grâce—the speech that would condemn Robespierre's enemies on the Committee. But before he had caught his first breath, he was interrupted by another deputy who condemned Robespierre as a tyrant. Another deputy spoke and then another, in a carefully orchestrated chorus of condemnation. Saint-Just was pushed from the platform.

At first Robespierre was too shocked to say anything. When he finally found his voice, he was shouted down and jeered at. Enraged, Robespierre sputtered furiously, unable to speak. "The blood of Danton is choking him!" cried a deputy. Someone called for the arrest of the Convention's president. Before Robespierre knew what was happening, he and his followers were surrounded by guards and rushed out of the hall. Realizing no prison would take these still-powerful men, the conspirators had them detained at the mayor's house.

Robespierre and his cohorts meet their end on July 27, 1794 after one of the swiftest falls in modern political history. Robespierre, his head bandaged from a self-inflicted wound, receives a parting kiss from a companion. Note the condemned man nearby geting a last-minute haircut to present a clean neck for the blade. (The Bettmann Archive)

The alarm went out and the Commune sprang into action. Insurrection was in the air. Robespierre himself, however, had stripped the sans-culottes of their power. With Hébert gone, the Commune was leaderless and no more united than the Committee of Public Safety. Robespierre had his supporters and detractors among the people, but many now felt indifferent to his fate. In the end, only 13 of the 48 of the Commune's sections sent troops to save the Robespierrists. Yet they were strong enough to liberate the captives.

Robespierre and his men barricaded themselves in City Hall, protected by a cordon of Commune soldiers, who waited anxiously for their next orders. But the Convention's violent denunciation of him had left Robespierre stunned. He had been so preoccupied with his own plans that the plot against him caught him completely by surprise. The once-masterful strategist seemed strangely paralyzed, unable to act. As precious hours passed, the Robespierrists did nothing. Leaderless, the Commune men lost their resolve and began to disband. By 2 A.M. City Hall was defenseless. The Convention's troops marched in. As they prepared to storm the building, a man fell from a window at their feet. It was Robespierre's brother Augustin, who had thrown himself from a window. He lay there with a broken leg.

The sight that greeted the soldiers inside was no less pathetic. The hapless Couthon lay moaning at the bottom of a flight of stairs, having fallen in a vain attempt to escape. Another Robespierrist, La Bas, had committed suicide. Robespierre himself had botched his attempt at a dignified exit. The bullet he fired had missed his mouth and shattered his jaw. The only member of the group in one piece was the strangely calm Saint-Just, who surrendered without resistance.

In the early-morning hours, the broken men were taken to the Tuileries. Robespierre, groaning with pain, was placed on a table where he lay for six hours as the Convention debated what to do with him. A pamphlet published soon after described how low the great leader had fallen:

> . . . they laid his head on a box full of mouldy ration bread. . . .He did not move, but he was breathing heavily, and put his right hand

Maximilien Robespierre (1758-1794)

Robespierre, as this portrait shows, was an impeccable dresser. Although he lacked Danton's eloquence and Marat's passion, he exuded a curious charisma of his own. Women found him fascinating and vied to get a lock of his hair. (The New York Public Library Picture Collection)

A visitor to Paris today will look in vain for a public memorial to the Revolution's last great leader. Robespierre's only lasting legacy is the Reign of Terror, for which he has been vilified for 200 years.

Surely Robespierre was a butcher, but it should be remembered that he committed these terrible acts out of the highest ideals, without a thought to personal gain. It hardly excuses what he did, but it helps to understand this complicated, difficult man.

Robespierre felt the burden of responsibility early in life. The eldest of five children, he took over the raising of his siblings when his mother died in childbirth and his father abandoned the family. Although poor, he

on his forehead; clearly he was trying to hide his face; disfigured as he was, he still showed signs of vanity. . . . The surgeon said that the lower jaw was broken . . . During this operation, everyone offered his comments. When they put the bandage round his head, a man said, "Now they are crowning his majesty."

was bright and earned a scholarship to study law in Paris. In 1781 he returned to his native Arras to practice law. He quickly gained a reputation as an excellent legal mind and an eloquent writer of political essays. Robespierre's radical political philosophy was shaped by the writings of Rousseau, whom he worshiped.

Elected to the Estates-General in 1787, Robespierre was a small but radical voice for the Third Estate. His power gradually expanded, and within a few years he was elected president of the influential Jacobin Club. In the National Assembly, he voted for the king's death and called for a democratic republic.

Unlike his one-time friend Danton, Robespierre was not an easy man to like. He was something of a prig, had no sense of humor and never married. For some reason women found him fascinating, and he received marriage proposals by the score. In public he appeared cold and distant, although he could be warm and engaging among friends. Robespierre lacked the brilliance and appeal of other Revolutionary leaders, but his dedication to the Revolution and his unflagging honesty won him the respect of the people, who named him "the Incorruptible."

What finally did "corrupt" Robespierre was his inability to see people as individual human beings and not just a conglomerate of ideal citizens. The moral passion that fueled his life also blinded him to the reality around him. He failed to understand that the masses were more interested in full stomachs and a roof over their heads than in his lofty ideals. The "republic of virtue" Robespierre struggled to bring into being was stillborn. Morality could not be legislated, not even on the blade of the guillotine.

By 11 A.M. the verdict was in. Death for Robespierre and 22 of his followers. Eight hours later, Robespierre and his friends followed the path they had sent thousands down before them. The final indignity was performed by the executioner, who coolly ripped the paper bandage from Robespierre's jaw so no obstruction would come between his head and the guillotine. Thus the last utterance of the architect of the Terror was, appropriately, a shriek.

CHAPTER 9 NOTES

p. 83   "Any individual who usurps . . ." David Dowd, *The French Revolution*, p. 143.

p. 85   "He wore his usual light blue coat . . ." Richard Cobb and Colin Jones, *Voices of the French Revolution*, p. 224.

p. 85   "Look at the bastard . . ." Cobb and Jones, *Voices of the French Revolution*, p. 224.

pp. 87–88 ". . . they laid his head on a box . . ." Cobb and Jones, *Voices of the French Revolution*, pp. 232–233.

THE END OF
THE STORM

"[The French] need glory, the satisfaction of their vanity; but as for liberty, they know nothing about it . . . The nation needs a leader, a leader made illustrious by glory."
—Napoléon Bonaparte

For many historians, the death of Robespierre marks the end of the French Revolution. What follows is largely anticlimatic. There is much truth to this opinion, for by July 1794 the great leaders who had given the Revolution its meaning and direction were all gone. However, the next five years, while less dramatic, are important because they show what was lost and what was gained by the momentous events that preceded them.

The guillotine's grisly work did not end with Robespierre's last shriek. Within 24 hours of his execution, 80 more of his supporters went to their deaths. More executions of Robespierrists followed, but the bloodletting soon slowed to a trickle. The Reign of Terror was over. The doors of Paris's prisons were flung open, and thousands of prisoners were released—from conservative royalists to radical Hébertists. One by one the tools of the Terror were dismantled. The Committee of Public Safety was transformed into a harmless extension of the Convention. The Commune was broken into two committees with little power and the Revolutionary Tribunal was radically altered. New decrees made it a far more lenient court of justice. In November 1794 the Jacobin Club of Paris shut its doors for good.

The Convention resumed its former power but without strong leadership to guide it. The Thermidorians, it turned out, had no agenda for the future. They had destroyed Robespierre out of fear and jealousy, not any overriding moral conviction. Indeed, they were just as guilty of the Terror as Robespierre was, although they now found it in their best interests to heap all the blame upon him. The conspirators became moderates because it was the expedient thing to do. They were, above all, political animals.

As with any period of extremism, what followed Robespierre's "republic of virtue" was a harsh reaction to it. Middle-class people, including merchants and professionals, came out of their holes and started enjoying life again. The theaters, closed by Jacobin censors, were reopened, restaurants flourished,[1] and gambling houses did a brisk business. The city's night life had enough vice, sin and excess to set Robespierre spinning in his grave.

Fashion took a bizarre turn, reducing the Terror to a sick joke. Young people wore their hair cut short to resemble the shaved heads of the condemned and tied a red ribbon around their throats so no one would miss the point. Young men in outlandish clothes stalked the night streets of Paris armed with sticks weighed at one end with lead. Their favorite sport was bashing Jacobins and sans-culottes and smashing to bits busts of Jacobin heroes. These *jeunesse dorée* (gilded youth) were the sons of respectable middle-class families, many of whom had gone into hiding to escape conscription into the republican army.

A far more serious threat to the French republic was brewing in southeastern France. Returning émigrés, royalists and other counterrevolutionaries were seizing their moment of revenge. They struck back at their now-vulnerable Jacobin enemies with a savagery that earned them the name "White Terror," white being the color of the French monarchy.

---

1. Food became a major passion for the nouveaux riches of Paris. Haute cuisine was raised to a fine art, and many new dishes were invented. One of the most famous of these, still enjoyed today, was lobster thermidor.

By the spring of 1795, this new terror reached its peak. Lyon became a slaughterhouse once more, as imprisoned Jacobins were pulled from their cells and murdered. Lynch mobs were organized with such misleading names as "The Company of Jesus." These bloody reprisals continued for another two years throughout southern France's cities, towns and villages.

Keeping order was only one of the problems facing the Convention. The winter of 1794–95 was one of the coldest in a century. Famine and bitter cold held Paris in its grip. Many of the poor committed suicide rather than face a lingering death by starvation. Those who survived the winter rose up in protest against a do-nothing Convention. They marched on the Convention Hall crying for bread, but were quickly dispersed by the National Guard. Nearly two months later they rose up again, and this time a thousand sans-culottes were arrested. The moderates were once again on the defensive. Something had to be done to reestablish order and ensure the future of the state.

The royalists, of course, wanted a new king. Louis XVII, son of Louis XVI and Marie-Antoinette, had languished in prison until 1794, when the Jacobins had attempted to "reeducate" him under the stern tutelage of a sans-culotte cobbler named Simon. Simon's harsh treatment only worsened the pathetic boy's poor health, and he died of neglect in June 1795. Soon after, the child's uncle, the Comte de Provence, proclaimed himself Louis XVIII from the safety of a comfortable exile in Italy. But all his plotting to regain the throne came to nothing. Too much had happened in France to allow the monarchy to be reestablished, even a constitutional monarchy.[2]

To establish order, the Convention forged still another constitution for France. This one was vastly different from the two documents that had preceded it. The Jacobins' dream of equality for all was brushed aside, along with most of their democratic reforms. The right to private property and its protection was reinstated and the very word "revolutionary" was outlawed. Only Frenchmen of property now had the right to vote. A two-house legislature was set up and a new executive branch established. It consisted of five men called the Directory. Each director

---

2. The monarchy was brought back 35 years later in the "second revolution" that put Louis-Philippe, a constitutional monarch, on the throne.

had equal power, and the leadership rotated, so no one man could become more powerful than the others. The new government wanted no more Robespierres.

The Directory's ambitious goals were to replace "the chaos which always accompanies revolutions by a new social order . . . revive in-

The ridiculous pomposity of the Directory is captured in this period engraving of one of its members. The five-man Directory drained the Revolution of its vitality and idealism. Its weak, ineffectual government paved the way for the rise of Napoléon Bonaparte. (The Bettmann Archive)

dustry and commerce, stamp out speculation, revitalize the arts and sciences, reestablish public credit and restore plenty." It fell dismally short of almost all these goals. It wasn't entirely the Directory's fault. The country was exhausted from the traumatic events of the past seven years. The people were in no mood to make further sacrifices to their country. They wanted bread and jobs, and they wanted them now. Egged on by the royalists, the people of Paris rose up once more to vent their discontent with the new conservative government.

An ambitious 26-year-old brigadier general named Napoléon Bonaparte was given the task of defending the Convention from the mob's attack. This capable soldier ordered 40 cannon brought in from outside the city and set up around the Convention Hall in the Tuileries. The "Vendémiaire Rising," as it has come to be called, began on a crisp October morning. Every time the mob rushed to attack, the fire of the cannon drove them back. By early evening it was all over, and some 100 attackers were dead. General Bonaparte had won the day with a firm strategy and what he called a "whiff of grapeshot." The Convention was grateful but also concerned. The incident had clearly shown that the army was the only power left in France that could keep order.

To put Napoléon in his place and out of the way, the Convention sent him to Italy, one of the few countries France had not yet defeated on the battlefield. They expected him to fail, but Napoléon surprised them. He conquered the Italians in a series of masterful victories and divided the country into a number of small states. Next, Napoléon defeated the Austrians, leaving Great Britain as France's one remaining enemy on the battlefield. Napoléon's triumphs made him bolder. He was starting to act like an independent power, totally free from the rule of the Directory.

The time was coming when this committee of colorless men would need Napoléon's help just to stay in power. Returning émigrés and old royalists at home ran for office in the elections of 1797 and won seats in the Convention. This legislative body was now divided against itself—monarchists on one side, and republicans on the other. Napoléon sent one of his generals back to Paris to help oust the monarchists. The Directory gratefully accepted his help and proclaimed the results of the election invalid. In doing so they made a mockery of their own constitution.

Napoléon Bonaparte (1769–1821)

Still a teenager when the Bastille fell, Napoléon was in many ways a child of the Revolution. In him, the principles of The Rights of Man were both fulfilled and annihilated.

Napoléon was born into a titled family on the island of Corsica in the Mediterranean Sea. He attended military school in Paris and at 16 was commissioned as a second lieutenant of artillery. He returned to Corsica, but was expelled from the island by counterrevolutionaries. Napoléon joined the Revolution in France and led a bold assault on Toulon in 1793, freeing the city from the British. This heroism won him promotion to brigadier general. After Robespierre's

The dashing young Napoléon shown here looks more like a Revolutionary hero than the emperor of France he will later become. He first came to attention when he took the city of Toulon back from the British in 1793 and was promoted from a major to a brigadier general. (The New York Public Library Picture Collection)

There was little now to stop Napoléon from taking over France. But he bided his time. The government ordered him to attack their last foreign enemy—England. As bold a strategist as ever, Napoléon decided to strike the enemy at its back door. In the summer of 1798 he invaded Egypt, a British colony, in hopes of sealing off England's Asian empire to the east. For once, Napoléon had erred. The British commander, Lord Nelson, met the French fleet at the mouth of the Nile

fall, however, Napoléon fell out of favor and was briefly imprisoned. His dispersal of the mob at the Tuileries made him a hero all over again. As his victories against France's enemies continued and his popularity increased, Napoléon's ambitions grew.

After becoming First Consul in 1799, Napoléon set out to incorporate the Revolution's achievements into France's legal and political system. He created the Napoleonic Code out of a tangle of overlapping local legal systems and standardized the nation's laws. He founded the Bank of France and put the nation on a firm and secure financial base for the first time in decades. He finished off the last vestiges of feudalism by making all civil and military promotions on the basis of merit alone and not class.

Napoléon did all these things, but he also made himself an emperor whose power was more absolute than that of Louis XVI. He led his people to glory in a war of conquest that brought most of Europe under French rule. But Napoléon overreached himself when he invaded Russia and started down the long road to defeat. After giving up his throne in 1814, he rallied his troops once more, but met defeat again at the battle of Waterloo against the British. Exiled to the island of St. Helena, Napoléon died a bitter, thwarted man in 1821.

As controversial today as he was in life, Napoléon has been labeled both a tyrant and a liberator. He gave France an empire instead of a republic, but in building his empire, he kept many of the lasting values of the Revolution alive for generations to come.

River and wiped it out. Napoléon had lost his vital lines of communication and was forced to concede the war. He quietly left his army and returned to France.

Napoléon was too great a man to be cowed by his first military defeat. His adventures in Egypt had been an exciting interlude in a drab year for the French people. The exotic campaign, heightened by the astonishing discovery of the Rosetta Stone by scholars accompanying

Napoléon's expedition, captured the public's imagination and whetted the French people's appetite for an empire of their own.[3] Napoléon was greeted in Paris as a conquering hero.

The Directory and the Convention were not happy to see him, but an older and wiser voice from the revolutionary past welcomed Napoléon with open arms. The Abbé Sieyès had pointed the way to revolution in his pamphlet "What Is the Third Estate?" in 1789; now he was pointing France in a very different direction. Sieyès believed the Directory's days were numbered and that new leadership was needed. It had to come from the only institution left with any power—the army. To inspire, in Sieyès's own words, "confidence from below," the country needed "authority from above."

The one man who had proven capable of exercising such authority was Napoléon Bonaparte. Sieyès shared his plan with the general, who had been thinking along the same lines. The Convention denounced Napoléon for the Egyptian defeat, and he responded by siezing power in a bold coup d'état on November 9, 1799. The Directory was dissolved and replaced by a Consulate composed of three consuls—Sieyès and Napoléon, plus one other. Napoléon was the first and most powerful consul. In effect, he had become master of France.

On December 15 Napoléon unveiled a new constitution to the people. "Citizens," he proclaimed, "the Revolution is established upon its original principles. It is over." And so the French Revolution ended, as it had begun, with one master as the head of state.

CHAPTER 10 NOTES

p. 91   "[The French] need glory . . ." Susan Banfield, *The Rights of Man, The Reign of Terror*, p. 188.

pp. 94–95 "The chaos which always accompanies . . ." Banfield, *The Rights of Man*, p. 185.

p. 98   Citizens, the Revolution is established . . ." N. S. Pratt, *The French Revolution*, p. 118.

---

3. This stone slab bore the same inscription in three languages, including Greek and Egyptian hieroglyphics. By using the known Greek language, scholars were able to decode the hieroglyphics for the first time.

THE LONG
LEGACY

"In such an atmosphere there can be only one kind of tactic,
the tactic of Danton: Audacity, audacity, and again audacity!"
—Joseph Stalin

For those fortunate Frenchmen and women who had survived ten tempest-tossed years of revolution, the rise of Napoléon as emperor of France might well have been the final disillusionment. Had all the rhetoric, the struggle, the hundreds of thousands of lives sacrificed in war, insurrection and terror, all been for this—the establishment of an absolute dictator?

The ideals of "liberty, equality and fraternity" survived Napoléon. They led in time to three more "French revolutions" in the 19th century, all less bloody and far briefer than the original. The first two revolutions—in 1830 and 1848—ended in failure, with the same kind of conservative backlash that occurred after Thermidor in 1794. But the revolution of 1870 ended in the establishment of a permanent democracy in the form of the Third Republic of France.

One does not have to look to 1870 to see the revolutionary tree of liberty bearing fruit, however. In that Napoléonic year of 1799 France

The French Revolution continues to exert a hold on the imagination of the French, as seen by the avenging angel's stirring call to arms in this detail from the Arc de Triomphe. (The Bettmann Archive)

was already a very different place from what it had been before the storming of the Bastille. The absolute monarchy and divine right of kings was gone forever. Although kings and emperors would be crowned again in France, they would rule by the will of the people, not their own whim. Those who tried to rule differently would be quickly swept out of power. Feudalism and the rigid society that it established was also gone. The privilege of the nobility and the church was ended. Money and merit were the new means of advancement. Those with ability and a good business sense could improve their lot in life, no matter how low their station. The laws were the same for all French peoples as legislated by a freely elected assembly and enforced by an independent court system.

Of course, reform went only so far. The democratic utopia envisioned by the Jacobins was not to be fulfilled. The lot of the poor was improved but poverty remained. For the first time the peasants had the opportunity to buy land, and some prospered. However, the working class of the cities were largely exploited as the Industrial Revolution got under way. The church returned to favor and regained its status in society, but without the vast power and wealth it had under the old regime. Those who benefited the most from the Revolution were those in the middle class—merchants, financiers, politicians and military men—who became, in a sense, the new aristocracy.

The Revolution had transformed France, but it also transformed Europe. Initially judged a failure when compared with the American Revolution, the French Revolution proved in the long run to be just as influential, perhaps more so. The republican army was the first truly national army of Europe, fighting for love of country and national ideals and not for money or the glory of a king. French soldiers exported nationalism to the countries they fought against, a process that was accelerated during the Napoleonic Wars. Every country Napoléon conquered caught the fever of nationalism and eventually revolted against the established order. Italy, Ireland, Belgium, Switzerland, Poland and the German states were all ablaze with rebellion. Some revolutions succeeded, others failed. But Europe would never be the same again.

The French Revolution inspired not only a social and political revolution but a cultural one as well. Romanticism, the triumph of feeling over reason and the individual over society, exploded in the arts. It was eloquently expressed in the poetry of Wordsworth and Byron in England, the music of Beethoven in Germany, the art of David in France and later the writings of Emerson and Thoreau in the United States. Western civilization suddenly saw itself anew, freed from the bonds of the past, ready to face a new dawn of limitless possibilities.

But there was also a dark side to the legacy. The class warfare waged under the urging of Marat and Hébert was an inspiration to German political theorist Karl Marx, the father of communism. Communism hoped to succeed where the French Revolution failed, creating a system of government where workers would unite and overthrow their capitalist bosses. Vladimir Lenin, an ardent Marxist and revolutionary, formed the Bolshevik Party and took over Russia during the Russian Revolution of 1917. The Russian Revolution is in some ways a 20th-century replay of the French Revolution. Czar Nicholas II, like Louis XVI, was a weak and ineffectual ruler, heir to a dying dynasty. The

Provisional Government that replaced the czar was as incompetent as the Girondists, while the Bolsheviks under Lenin were as ruthless and pragmatic as the Jacobins. Similar to Robespierre's "republic of virtue," Lenin's worker state quickly degenerated into a totalitarian state, where a small elite dictated the lives of the majority.

The Communist leaders found an inspiring model in the French Revolution. They even derived their vocabulary from the earlier revolt. "Citizen," the universal form of address in revolutionary France, became "Comrade" in Communist Russia. The chilling euphemisms of the Committee of Public Safety echoed in such Bolshevik terms as "liquidate" (kill) and "enemies of the people" (anyone you want to liquidate). The French Revolution's use of propaganda, parades and other commemorative events to cement the power of the new state was raised to a high art by Lenin's even more ruthless successor, Joseph Stalin. The Reign of Terror would find its 20th-century equivalent in Stalin's purges of the 1930s. The genocide inflicted on the Vendéans and other counterrevolutionary "traitors" foreshadowed the horrors of Stalin's gulag and Hitler's concentration camps.

Today the great and terrible legacy lives on. The Revolution is alive in the fanatical commitment of political terrorists for whom no price is too high to pay for an ideal. But it also lives in the rebirth of freedom in Eastern Europe, where the same desire for freedom that drove the French have helped topple Communist regimes. Historian Simon Schama has even gone so far as to compare the breakup of the Soviet Union in 1991 with the French Revolution. "Like the Soviet Union, the monarchy of Louis XVI was an overextended empire, trying to be a global power while failing the elementary test of legitimacy: feeding its people," he writes. ". . . The regime ultimately collapsed from its ruler's fatal inconsistency in the application of reform and his reluctance to embrace representative institutions that could give these changes a democratic sanction." Schama hopes, as we all do, that the second Russian Revolution will go the way of the American Revolution and not the French.

In 1989 the French celebrated the 200th anniversary of their revolution with spectacles, parades and fireworks. The entire world joined in the celebration, for in the two centuries since the fall of the Bastille, the French Revolution has become part of our heritage too. From history's long perspective, we can now see that the French Revolution marked the emergence of the modern world, embodying humanity's vast potential for both constructive change and self-destruction.

CHAPTER 11 NOTES

p. 99   "In such an atmosphere . . ." Robert Payne, *The Rise and Fall of Stalin*, p. 217.

p. 102   "Like the Soviet Union . . ." Simon Schama, *The New York Times*, September 5, 1991.

CHRONOLOGY

1762 • Jean-Jacques Rousseau's *The Social Contract* is published.

1774 • Louis XVI becomes king of France.

1775–83 • The American Revolution is fought and won by the American colonists with aid from the French.

1786

August • Minister Charles de Calonne's reform for taxes is presented to and rejected by the Assembly of Notables.

1788 • The Revolt of the Nobility takes place. Parlement denounces the king as a despot.

1789

May 5 • The Estates-General opens at Versailles.

June 17 • The Third Estate declares itself the National Assembly.

June 20 • The Assembly takes the Tennis Court Oath, vowing to stay together until a constitution is established.

June 23 • Count Mirabeau defies the king's order to leave the hall after the Royal Session.

July 11 • The king dismisses his reform-minded minister Jacques Necker.

July 14 • The Bastille is stormed and taken over by the people of Paris.

August 4	•	The Assembly begins to abolish the laws of feudalism.
August 27	•	The Declaration of the Rights of Man and the Citizen is issued.
October 5–6	•	The women of Paris march on Versailles to protest conditions and bring the king back to Paris.
1790	•	Political clubs, including that of the Jacobins and the Girondists, begin to proliferate.
July 12	•	Clergy are required to take an oath to the new constitution.
1791		
April 2	•	Mirabeau dies.
June 21	•	The royal family attempts to leave France but is caught at Varennes and brought back to Paris.
July 17	•	The National Guard under Lafayette kills more than 50 protesters in the Champ de Mars Massacre.
September 14	•	The king swears to uphold the new constitution.
October 1	•	The new Legislative Assembly meets.
Fall	•	The Girondists begin their climb to power.
1792		
April 20	•	France declares war on Austria.
June 20	•	Sans-culottes invade the Tuileries Palace and force the king to drink to the health of the nation.
August	•	Lafayette is captured by the Austrians after fleeing France.
August 9	•	The Paris Commune is formed.
August 10	•	The king is overthrown following a bloody battle at the Tuileries.
late August	•	The guillotine is unveiled in Paris.
September 2–6	•	Half of all the prisoners in Paris are slaughtered in the September Massacres.
September 20	•	The French army wins a decisive victory against the Prussians at Valmy.

September 21	•	The National Convention meets for the first time and abolishes the monarchy, proclaiming France a republic.
October	•	Georges Danton resigns from the largely Girondist Executive Council and joins forces with the more radical Robespierre.
December 11	•	The trial of Louis XVI begins.

1793

January 21	•	Louis XVI is executed.
Winter	•	France goes to war against England, the Netherlands and Spain.
March	•	Counterrevolution begins in the Vendée.
April 6	•	The Jacobins consolidate their power by establishing the Revolutionary Tribunal and the Committee of Public Safety.
May	•	Jean-Paul Marat goes on trial and is acquitted by the Tribunal, a major setback for the Girondists.
May 29– June 2	•	The Girondists fall from power and their leaders are arrested.
July 10	•	Danton is discredited and leaves the Committee of Public Safety.
July 13	•	Marat is assassinated by Charlotte Corday.
July 27	•	Robespierre becomes a member of the Committee of Public Safety.
September	•	The Reign of Terror begins.
October	•	The Vendéans lose their last major battle.
October 16	•	Marie-Antoinette is executed.
Fall– Winter	•	France is triumphant over foreign enemies.
December	•	The Dantonists call for a lessening of the Terror.

1794

| February | • | The Jacobins abolish slavery in French colonies and distribute the property of émigrés to the poor. |

March	•	The radical Hébert and his followers are executed.
March 31	•	Danton is arrested and charged with anti-Jacobinism.
April 6	•	Danton and his followers are executed.
June 8	•	Robespierre presides over the Festival of the Supreme Being.
June 10	•	The Great Terror begins.
July 27	•	Robespierre is denounced as a tyrant in the Convention.
July 28	•	Robespierre, Saint-Just, Couthon and others are executed.
August	•	The Terror ends, the power of the Committee of Public Safety and Revolutionary Tribunal is broken, prisoners are released.
Fall	•	The "gilded youth" persecute Jacobins and are part of a conservative backlash.

1795

May 20	•	The sans-culottes revolt in Paris but are put down by the National Guard.
Spring	•	The White Terror, a counterrevolutionary movement, reaches its peak in the provinces.
June	•	Louis XVII dies of neglect. His uncle declares himself Louis XVIII.
August	•	A new constitution, more conservative than its predecessors, is proclaimed.
October	•	The Directory takes over as the executive power in the government.
	•	The Vendémiaire Rising is put down by Napoléon Bonaparte.
1796–97	•	Napoléon conducts his successful Italian campaign.
1798	•	Napoléon fights the British in Egypt but is defeated by Lord Nelson and returns to France.

1799

| November 5 | • | Napoléon expels the Convention from office. |

November 9–10	•	The Directory is replaced by three consuls. Napoléon is made first consul.
December 15	•	Napoléon unveils a new constitution and declares the Revolution over.

FURTHER READING

NONFICTION BOOKS

Banfield, Susan. *The Rights of Man, The Reign of Terror: The Story of the French Revolution* (New York: J.B. Lippincott, 1989). A clearly written, attractively designed history for young adults.

Blanc, Olivier. *Last Letters: Prisons and Prisoners of the French Revolution* (New York: Farrar, Straus & Giroux, 1987). A fascinating collection of actual letters written by the condemned during the Terror, with an informative commentary on prison life during the Revolution.

Cobb, Richard, and Jones, Colin. *Voices of the French Revolution* (Topsfield, Mass.: Salem House, 1988). An indispensable volume, lavishly illustrated, that skillfully interweaves historical narrative with primary source material.

Dowd, David L. *The French Revolution* (New York: American Heritage, 1965). Part of the Horizon Caravel Book series for young adults. An excellent, well-illustrated introduction to the period.

Eimerl, Sarel. *Revolution! France 1789–1794* (Boston: Little, Brown, 1967). Highlights major moments of the Revolution with dramatic flair.

Robiquet, Jean. *Daily Life in the French Revolution* (New York: Macmillan, 1965). An intriguing social history of what life was like for the ordinary person during the Revolutionary period.

Pratt, N.S. *The French Revolution* (New York: John Day, 1970). Part of the Young Historian Books series. This straightforward history is most interesting for its sympathetic portrayal of Robespierre.

Schama, Simon. *Citizens: A Chronicle of the French Revolution* (New York: Knopf, 1989). The best single volume in English on the Revolution to appear in years. It is fascinating in its detail and breath of scholarship. A long read, but well worth the effort.

FICTION, POETRY AND DRAMA ABOUT THE FRENCH REVOLUTION

Buchner, Georg. *Danton's Death* (with two other plays) (Oxford, England: Oxford University Press, 1988, paper). Written in 1835, this starkly realistic play about one of the Revolution's legends was written by one of Germany's greatest dramatists who was only 23 when he died.

Carlyle, Thomas. *The French Revolution* (Oxford, England: Oxford University Press, 1989). Although written as history, critics consider this an epic drama illustrating the great Scottish prose writer's theory that history is made by heroes.

Coleridge, Samuel Taylor. "France: An Ode" in *Coleridge: The Laurel Poetry Series* (New York: Dell, 1959, paper). A dramatic poem about the Revolution by one of England's great Romantic poets.

Dickens, Charles. *A Tale of Two Cities* (New York: Bantam, 1989, paper). The most famous novel about the French Revolution and one of Dickens's most popular books.

Orczy, Emmuska. *The Scarlet Pimpernel* (New York: Penguin, 1989, paper). A rousing adventure story about a young Englishman who disguised himself to rescue French aristocrats from the Terror.

Sabatini, Raphael. Scaramouche (Mattituck, N.Y.: Amerean, 1976). Another classic adventure about a wandering actor caught up in the Revolution.

FILMS AVAILABLE ON VIDEO

Danton. Directed by Andrezj Wajda. 1983. A powerful film from Poland about the final battle of wills between Danton and Robespierre, with a riveting performance by French actor Gerard Depardieu as Danton.

Marat/Sade. Directed by Peter Brook, adapted from the play by Peter Weiss. 1966. This brilliant film depicts Marat's assassination as performed 15 years after the Revolution in a French insane asylum under the direction of the Marquis de Sade. The debate between Sade and Marat on the nature of man and revolution is exhilarating.

Napoleon. Directed by Abel Gance. 1927. One of the silent screen's greatest epics by a legendary French director. The title is misleading since much of the film is about the Reign of Terror and deals with Napoléon only as a young military cadet and soldier. Reissued in 1981 with a new score by Carmine Coppola, father of director Francis.

Orphans of the Storm. Directed by D.W. Griffith. 1922. This melodramatic story of two sisters caught up in the Terror is less than historically accurate but is vividly told by the first great American film director.

Start the Revolution Without Me. Directed by Bud Yorkin. 1970. Gene Wilder and Donald Sutherland are two sets of twins in this entertaining comedy set during the French Revolution.

INDEX

Boldface numbers indicate special treatment of topic.
Italic numbers indicate illustrations and captions.

A

American Revolution 3, 20, 52, 101, 105
Ami du peuple, L' (newspaper) 64–65
"Angel of Death" *See* Saint-Just, Louis Antoine Léon de
Arc de Triomphe *100*
Artois, Count of 12
Assembly of Notables 4, 6, 105
atheism 75–76, 78, 84
Austria 31–34, 57, 60

B

Bailly, Jean-Sylvain 11–12, 20, 27
Bank of France 97
Bastille, fall of the 13–18, *15*, 19, 27, 52, 96, 100, 102, 105
Bastille Day 18
Baudot, Marc-Antoine 85
Beethoven, Ludwig van 101
Belgium 34, 56, 60, 101
Bolsheviks 101–102
Bonaparte, Napoléon **96–97**
  constitution 98
  coup d'état 98
  David and 39
  Directory 93–95
  Egypt campaign 96, 109
  as emperor 99
  exile of 97
  as first consul 97–98, 109
  Italian campaign 95, 108
  Lafayette and 55
  Napoleonic Code 97
  nationalism 101
  on need for strong leader 91
  Russia campaign 97

Vendémiaire Rising 95, 108
Waterloo battle 97
Bouille, Marquis de 25
Bourbons 1
Breteuil, Louis de 13
Brienne, Loménie de 4
Brissot, Jacques Pierre 31
Burke, Edmund 53–54, 56
Byron, Lord 101

C

Caesar, Julius 8
calendar 76–77
Calonne, Charles Alexandre de 4, 105
capital punishment
  abolition of in France 47
  guillotine as instrument of 46–47
Carnot, Lazore 75, 84–85
Champs de Mars massacre 27–28, 54, 106
Choiseul, Duke of 26
Christianity, attack on *See* de-Christianization
Clinton, De Witt 57
Club of 1789 23
Collot d'Herbois, Jean-Marie 83–84
Committee of Public Safety
  creation of 61, 107
  Danton career cut short 68, 107
  Danton trial 78–80
  dismantling of 91–92, 108
  dissension among members 84
  food shortages 78
  foreign wars 75
  Hébert attacks on 73, 78
  Reign of Terror 70
  Robespierre downfall 87

Thermidor, plot of 85
Third Estate
    doubling of number of deputies for 8
    and French society 6
    Mirabeau election to 29
    National Assembly emergence from 9–
        13, 105
    plight of 5
    Robespierre as voice for 89
Third Republic 99
Thoreau, Henry David 101
"Tribune of the People" *See* Mirabeau,
    Comte de
tricolor 21
tricoteuses 72
Tuileries Palace 23, 36–37, 52, 106
Turgot, Robert 3

U

United States of America 52, 56

V

Valmy, battle of 43–44, 60, 107

Varennes, flight to 25–27, *26*, 106
Vendée revolt 59–60, 73–75, *74*, 107
Vendémiaire Rising 95, 108
Verdun, battle of 42
Versailles, Palace of 1, 8, 21–23, *22*
Voltaire (François Marie Arouet) 3, 14, 75

W

"War Song of the Army of the Rhine" *See*
    "Marseillaise, La"
Washington, George 52, 54, 56–57
Waterloo, battle of 55, 97
Westermann, François-Joseph 73
What Is The Third Estate? (pamphlet) 9,
    98
White Terror 92, 108
Whitridge, Arnold 56
Wordsworth, William 101

Y

Yorktown, battle of 55
Young, Arthur 13